NEW Wide Range Readers
GREEN BOOK 6

Fred J. Schonell
Phyllis Flowerdew

Oliver & Boyd

Acknowledgments

We are grateful to the following for supplying photographs and giving permission for their use:
All-Sport/Tony Duffy, p. 141; BBC Hulton Picture Library/ Bettmann Archive, p. 105; Austin J. Brown (Aviation Picture Library), pp. 132, 133; Colorsport, p. 142; Daily Telegraph Colour Library, p. 28; A. F. Kersting, p. 29; E. D. Lacey, p. 137; The Mansell Collection, p. 91; Picturepoint, London, *cover*; Popperfoto, p. 125; S. & G. Press Agency Ltd, p. 143 (foot); Sporting Pictures (UK) Ltd, p. 143 (top).

Illustrated by Peter Cornwell, Terry Gabbey, Nicholas Hewetson, Harry Horse, Annabel Large, Tony Morris, Trevor Parkin and David Simon.

Oliver & Boyd
Addison Wesley Longman Limited
Edinburgh Gate
Harlow
Essex CM20 2JE

An Imprint of Longman Group UK Ltd

First published 1953
Second edition 1965
Third edition 1976
Fourth edition 1985
Eleventh impression 1996

© Phyllis Flowerdew and the Executors of the late Sir Fred J. Schonell 1965, 1985 (Except 'The Flying East Africans' © Anne Forsyth 1985.)

All rights reserved; no part of this publication may be reproduced, stored in a retrieval system, or transmitted in any form or by any means, electronic, mechanical, photocopying, recording, or otherwise without either the prior written permission of the Publishers or a licence permitting restricted copying in the United Kingdom issued by the Copyright Licensing Agency Ltd, 90 Tottenham Court Road, London, W1P 9HE.

ISBN 0 05 003754 4

Produced by Longman Singapore Publishers Pte Ltd
Printed in Singapore

The publisher's policy is to use paper manufactured from sustainable forests.

Preface

The Wide Range Readers are planned to provide graded reading practice for junior school children. Because children of 7–11 have a wide range of reading needs and attainments, there are three parallel series—Blue, Green and Red books—to provide plenty of material to suit the interests and reading ages of every child.

Books 1–4 are graded by half yearly reading ages, for use by appropriate groups within a class. Book 1 should provide an easy read for children with a reading age of about $7-7\frac{1}{2}$. Children with reading ages below 7 are recommended to use the Wide Range Starters.

The controlled vocabulary of the series makes the books suitable for the following reading ages:

$6\frac{1}{2}-7$	**Starter Books**—Blue, Green and Red
$7-7\frac{1}{2}$	**Book 1**—Blue, Green and Red
$7\frac{1}{2}-8$	**Book 2**—Blue, Green and Red
$8-8\frac{1}{2}$	**Book 3**—Blue, Green and Red
$8\frac{1}{2}-9$	**Book 4**—Blue, Green and Red
$9+$	**Book 5**—Blue, Green and Red
$10+$	**Book 6**—Blue, Green and Red
$11+$	**Book 7**—Red only
$12+$	**Book 8**—Red only

Contents

page

5	Flying Doctor
22	The Jester's Church
30	Gold at Silver Grass
54	Kek Attacks
68	Les Pauvres Petits
90	A Cinderella
92	A Bargain
106	A Visit to the Moon
115	The Girl Who Loved Music
126	The Story of Parachutes
136	The Flying East Africans

Flying Doctor

It was five o'clock in the morning, at Kallaloola, five hundred kilometres from anywhere.

Judy, Gareth and Sheila had been awake most of the night, for Mother was very ill, and there was no one to help them. Kallaloola was a dry and dusty outpost of Australia. No one ever passed it except occasional stockmen and cattle drovers; and Father was away for six or seven weeks at a time.

"Five o'clock," said Gareth.

"Another whole hour till six," murmured Sheila.

At six o'clock they would be able to contact the Flying Doctor by radio, and even if he couldn't come to the house, he would be able to tell them what to do.

The children were so worried about Mother, and so impatient for the time to pass that they didn't hear the sound of horses' hooves outside, so they were startled suddenly by a loud beating at the door.

They looked at each other with wide, frightened eyes, for sleepless nights had made them strained and nervous.

"Who can it be?" they whispered, almost afraid to move. Seconds slipped silently by, and no one ventured to open the door.

"Come on," said Judy, the eldest, "we'll all go," and she led the way, just as the banging started anew.

"All right," called Gareth with a show of bravery to the person outside. "We're coming."

He and Sheila peered over their sister's shoulder as she opened the door, a crack at a time.

"Oh!" exclaimed Judy in relief. "It's Allawa!"

Allawa was an Aborigine who worked on the ranch, and he stood panting and breathless in the doorway.

"Oh, Allawa," said Sheila, flinging the door wide, "you terrified us! Mother's ill and—"

She stopped, knowing by the look on his face that Allawa had come with bad news.

"What is it?" asked Judy in fear.

"Boss—he bad fall—over river. Boss, he lie down by trees."

In his halting English he explained. Father's horse had thrown him the previous evening, and he was badly injured. Allawa had managed to carry him through the bush for several kilometres in the darkness, leading the horses at the same time, but it had taken him many hours, and he had decided at last that it would be wiser to come for help. He had left Father just beyond the river bed in the shade of some bushes, and he had ridden on through the night alone. He explained exactly where Father was lying, to the east of a coolabah tree, where the bushes were widely scattered.

"Radio," said Allawa finally. "Call Flying Doctor."

The children listened to his story in silence. Then they besieged him with questions and told him about Mother.

"You must be tired and hungry," said Sheila suddenly. "Rest on the veranda, and I'll bring you some food."

By the time Allawa had eaten, it was still scarcely twenty past five.

"Wait and hear what the Flying Doctor says before you go back," advised Gareth. "Oh, I wish it were six o'clock."

Fearful that somehow six o'clock might slip by unnoticed, the children took the old watch of Grandfather's by which they knew the time, and stood impatiently round the pedal radio.

It was only the pedal radio that kept them in touch with the outside world, giving them not only wireless programmes but opportunities to speak with neighbours a hundred and sixty kilometres away—connecting them not only with the news buzzing from outpost to outpost but—with the Flying Doctor service.

So, as the hands of Grandfather's watch moved to six o'clock, Judy sat at the pedal radio, generating power with the movement of her feet, pedalling as if life depended on it, which indeed it did.

She was soon through to the operator at the base station, telling in an anxious voice of Mother's illness and Father's accident.

"Stand by for a few minutes," said the operator, for he had to take a number of calls, and then connect people with the Flying Doctor in order of the urgency of their cases. It seemed hours to the children before they heard the Flying Doctor's voice.

"Doctor," said Judy, hesitating a little because of the importance of her message. "It's Judy West calling from Kallaloola. Everything has happened at once. Mother's been ill for several days—her chest hurts and she can hardly breathe—and now we've learnt that Father's badly injured 'way out in the bush. His horse stumbled and threw him. Father can't move. Allawa

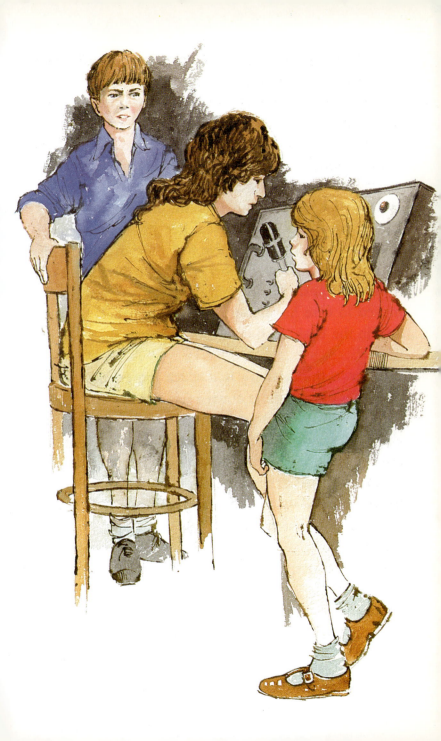

came on horseback from beyond the river to tell us about the accident." Her voice trailed on anxiously, describing the position as nearly as possible.

"Right, Judy," replied the doctor. "Now, get paper and a pencil, and listen carefully, will you?"

Gareth thrust pencil and paper into Judy's hands, and he and Sheila clustered nearer.

"See that your mother is warmly wrapped up," continued the doctor. "Prop her up with as many pillows as you can find. Give her a hot drink and one of the tablets in Box Number X3 of your Flying Doctor medicine chest. Now, your father; he must not be moved in case he should be injured further. You say he's in the bush. Is there a landing place there for my plane?"

"Allawa thinks there is a space big enough, if we smooth it out and chop down a few odd bushes."

"All right. I've to see another patient first, but I'll land near your father about midday. Is there someone you can send to clear the landing ground, and to take medicine to ease his pain till I can get there?"

Judy glanced up at Gareth and Sheila.

"Yes," she answered.

"You must also light a smoky fire to direct me. Now write down these numbers for the medicine."

In a few minutes the instructions were completed, and the conversation was over. Once more Kallaloola was cut off from the world, five hundred kilometres from anywhere.

The children understood well enough what they had to do. Judy must stay and look after Mother, while Gareth and Sheila must ride back with Allawa to the place where Father was lying alone. Hastily Judy made up the medicine while Gareth and Sheila packed food, water, two blankets, two choppers and a saw on to the horses.

"Ready, Allawa," they called. "Goodbye, Judy."

"Goodbye," said Judy, and she stood at the door watching them ride into the dusty distance. Then she made Mother comfortable, gave her the drink and the tablet, and waited while she dozed into unconsciousness. A moment later she saw that it was raining. Rain! It hadn't rained for more than a year, and it had to rain today!

* * * * * *

Meanwhile Gareth and Sheila and Allawa rode on, driving their horses along the trail that Allawa had left earlier. Already the marks of the horse shoes were half hidden by sand and dust, but Allawa's sense of direction was unfailing.

Then suddenly, even before the house was out of sight, a strange, cold shadow covered the earth. Rain! It was raining! For a moment Gareth and Sheila were excited and happy, for they loved and longed for rain, and it came so seldom. Then, as it drenched their clothes and poured down their faces, they were filled with dismay. Rain would only make things more difficult for Father.

"Well!" exclaimed Gareth. "Of all days in the year, it has to rain today!"

When it rained around Kallaloola, it certainly rained properly. It simply fell from the skies, so that in an unbelievably short time the ground was a swamp, and myriads of small, swift streams rushed among the bushes. The horses slipped and splashed in the mud, and the way became much more difficult, so that progress was slowed down considerably. Rain poured

ceaselessly, yet the sun shone at the same time, so that moisture rose from the earth in great clouds of steam, obscuring everything but the swamps around.

On rode the three, wondering if Father was sheltered enough, wondering how Mother was, wondering what the time was, and how long the Flying Doctor would be.

Then the river came in sight.

"Oh!" gasped Gareth. "Look at it!"

In the night, when Allawa had crossed it, it had been a calm stream in a bed of sand. Now, swelled by rain and by swollen streams from earlier rain in the hills, it had become a raging torrent, rushing wildly on its way in a furious search for the sea.

Allawa made a gesture with his thin, brown fingers.

"Water, he come up. Big fella river," he said.

Well—if there was a river, it must be crossed and the only way of crossing it was to swim behind the horses, clinging on to their tails as the Aborigines did.

"The tablets for Father," murmured Sheila. "They *must* be kept dry."

"Oh, yes," said Gareth. "And the matches." Then he grinned and added, "I know." He wrapped them in a handkerchief folded cornerwise, and tied the handkerchief over his head and under his chin. Sheila laughed, even though she stood on the brink of the swirling waters.

In a moment horses and humans were swimming for their lives—Allawa, Sheila and Gareth, in a silent, struggling procession. It was like a nightmare. There were times when they seemed to make no progress at all. There were times when they felt certain that they would be swept away. Yet somehow, before long, all three stood safely dripping on the other side, panting and speechless in the lashing rain, smiling and ready for the next stage of the journey.

And not long afterwards Allawa led them to Father—still alive, but moaning with pain, and recognising no one.

"The medicine," said Sheila immediately, and with fear in her heart, she eased one of the tablets down his throat.

Had they come too late? For hours and hours now Father had been here alone without food and water—alone in the dark and the dawn, alone in the sun and the rain.

Even now the Flying Doctor might not be in time to save him.

The mist lifted a little allowing a glimpse of the surroundings.

"Oh, dear!" cried Sheila, looking at the scattered bushes. "There'll *never* be room for an aeroplane to land here."

"Yes, there will," answered Gareth confidently. "An aeroplane doesn't take up half as much room as you would think. We've only to chop down that group of bushes in the middle there."

Only to chop them down!

The children started with a will—but they seemed to chop and chop to little purpose.

"Allawa do it," said the Aborigine. "Children pick stones. Light fire for Doctor."

Allawa was much better at it than they were. He had lived long enough to know the knack of chopping through tough stems and hacking out roots. Sheila and Gareth picked up stones and smoothed the sandy earth.

Then they tried to light a fire.

"Difficult in this rain," exclaimed Sheila.

They dug a hollow and arranged sticks in a small

pyramid within it. Gareth had kept the matches dry, but the wood was wet, and the rain damped any sparks that tried to flicker into flame.

They tried and tried without success. Even Allawa couldn't get a fire to burn.

"What shall we do?" asked Gareth. "We *must* make a fire for signalling the Flying Doctor."

Sheila looked round almost as if she expected a newspaper and a bundle of dry wood to appear from somewhere. Bush, sand, wet sticks. Nothing else. How *could* they make a fire?

"I know! I know!" she cried suddenly. "Blankets."

They were still tied up in a bundle. The outer one was wet, but the inner one was dry.

"Seems awful to burn a good blanket," she added, "but it's the only thing to do."

Allawa tore the blanket into strips. Then he and the children crouched over the hollow, protecting it from the rain with their bodies. They pushed a piece of blanket among the sticks and held a lighted match to it. The flame flickered and caught the blanket. It crept doubtfully along the jagged edge and leapt a moment into life. It gave a spurt of enthusiasm or of despair. Then it went out.

"Again, again," encouraged Gareth.

Again they lit the blanket. Again it went out. Again they lit it. Once more the flame crept doubtfully along the edge. Once more it flickered and failed, and leapt again to life. Then it burned. It flared up, and the blanket was alight!

Now there was no time to lose. As the children fed the fire with each piece of blanket, they dried sticks at the same time, and still sheltered the fire with their bodies. Slowly, slowly it grew in strength.

Allawa worked feverishly, chopping bushes and bringing more and more fuel for the fire.

"Allawa will have cut more than a landing place by the time he's finished," smiled Gareth.

"It must be a smoky fire," said Sheila, standing back a minute from the heat. Allawa remarked that he would make it a smoky fire just before midday—though the children wondered how he would know midday was near—especially as the sun was hidden by clouds, and there was no other means of telling the time.

But Allawa knew, and just before midday he let the fire die down a little, until a long twist of grey smoke curled up into the sky—a signal for the Flying Doctor. Now there would not be long to wait. Rain still fell, but the clouds cleared a little, and Gareth gave a sudden shout and pointed upwards. There in the grey sky was a gleam of silver—the aeroplane of the Flying Doctor on its way to help.

Breathlessly the children waited. They watched the aeroplane circle above their heads. They lost sight of it in the clouds. They saw it appear again and then disappear, as if the Flying Doctor had been unable to find the smoke signal.

They waited. Rain fell steadily. Perhaps the clouds were too thick. Perhaps the Flying Doctor could not see clearly. Perhaps the landing ground was not big enough after all.

"There it is again," whispered Sheila. Again there was a flash of silver, and this time the aeroplane came lower and lower, with a zoom of engines and a whirr of propellers.

Allawa and the children ran back to Father, a little fearful that the aeroplane might descend upon them all.

Then it landed—gently, smoothly.

The Flying Doctor had arrived! He and his pilot stepped down from the plane. In a second the doctor was attending to Father, and the pilot was beside him with splints and bandages and a stretcher.

"Children," said the doctor, "I'll have to set a few bones—so perhaps you'd like to go and explore my aeroplane while I'm busy."

"Oh, yes!" cried Gareth and Sheila. "Yes, *please*."

Later the doctor and the pilot carried Father to the plane, and fitted the stretcher into its special place.

"He was in a bad way," said the doctor, "but he'll be

all right now. I'll fly him to the hospital, but as your mother is ill too, I'll call in and see her on the way. Is there a landing place at your home?"

"Oh, yes," answered Gareth proudly. "There's a proper runway always ready for emergencies."

"Perhaps Allawa will ride back with the horses," continued the doctor, "and perhaps you'd like to come in the plane with me. Would you?"

Would they! There was no need to answer. The children's shining eyes said "yes" plainly enough.

It was a week later—six o'clock in the morning at Kallaloola, five hundred kilometres from anywhere—time to contact the Flying Doctor.

Judy sat smiling at the pedal radio, pedalling with her feet to generate power. Gareth and Sheila stood beside her, just for the pleasure of hearing the Flying Doctor's voice.

Judy was soon through to the operator. Then she had to wait some time so that the urgent calls could go through first—calls from people with pedal radios at outposts in the desert, the bush, the swamps, the floods. There were inquiries about treatment for accidents, illnesses, diseases that, if neglected, would result in death. There were requests for the doctor from far and wide.

Then it was Judy's turn, and her voice was confident and happy.

"Doctor, Judy West calling from Kallaloola. Mother's feeling so much better. May she get up soon?"

"Not for a day or two yet," replied the doctor. "Continue the treatment, and give me a call in two days' time. Hospital reports that your father's doing fine, Judy."

"Oh, good, Doctor! Thank you for everything."

Judy, Gareth and Sheila glanced at each other and smiled. Then once again Kallaloola was cut off from the world, five hundred kilometres from anywhere.

The Jester's Church

Long ago, at the court of King Henry the First, there lived a jester, whose name was Rahere. Everyone loved him, for he was happy and bright and full of fun. He could play and sing. He could make up stories and tell jokes, and whenever he wished, he could make people laugh—from the smallest page boy to the King himself.

But in spite of all his fun, Rahere was a wise and clever man; and though he spent his days in making the rich laugh, he thought often of the poor beyond the palace gates. He sometimes wondered what he could do for them—the thin, ragged people who looked so hungry, and the small, shouting children who looked so cold. It would be good to do something to help them, for they needed help.

But it was more pleasant to live at the King's court, and to have fine clothes and plenty of money. It was more pleasant to live among bright colours and flashing jewels, and to hear people say,

"Rahere, play to us."

"Rahere, sing to us."

"Rahere, please make us laugh."

Then one day Rahere went on a journey to Rome, and while he was there he became ill.

"You must go to bed, Rahere," said his friends.

"Oh, no," he replied. "It's only a cold. I'll be better

tomorrow." But when the next day came, Rahere had a fever and was too weak to move, and by evening he was so ill that his friends feared he would die.

For many days he seemed to lie between life and death. He didn't see his friends come and go. He didn't hear their anxious whispers. He knew nothing at all until about a week later when he awoke to find himself alone.

He had been dreaming of the King's court, of fine clothes, bright colours and flashing jewels. He had heard music, and merry voices saying,

"Make us laugh, Rahere. Make us laugh." When he awoke, he looked round for these things. But this was not the court. Where could he be? Slowly he remembered. Of course—he was ill. England and the King's court were far away. He wondered how long he had been in bed.

"It's lucky that I'm rich," he thought, "for who would have nursed me if I had been poor?"

He thought of the ragged people in the small houses beyond the King's palace. What happened to those people when they were ill?

"If I get better," he murmured to himself, "I will use my money to build a hospital for the poor, and a church for the worship of God. I'll leave the King's court and the easy, carefree life of the palace. I'll work for the poor." Rahere closed his eyes and prayed,

"O God—make me well again, so that I may build a church for Thee, and a hospital for the poor." As he prayed he fell asleep, and while he slept, the fever left him.

*   *   *   *   *   *

So Rahere gradually grew stronger, until at last he was able to return to England. Then he went at once to the palace, and told the King of his illness and his promise. He asked to be allowed to leave the court so that he

could start to build the church and the hospital he had planned.

"You may go, Rahere," said the King. "It will be a strange thing indeed for a jester to build a church—but I'll give you my blessing and I'll give you the land to build upon. Where do you wish it to be?"

"I want to build at Smithfield in London," replied Rahere. "Ever since my illness left me, I've been wondering where I should build. Then last night Saint Bartholomew appeared to me in a dream and he told me to build at Smithfield."

"Smithfield," said the King. "You may certainly have that land. It's a marshy and desolate place. And who will help you to build? You'll need many men to labour."

"The people will help me themselves when they know that I'm making a church and a hospital for them. They will gladly give a little of their time, I'm sure."

So Rahere gave away his fine clothes. He said goodbye to the people he had known so long, and he left the palace where he had been so happy. Wearing only the simple, brown robe of a monk, he went to Smithfield. There he drained away the water from the marshy land and he dug the foundations, as he had planned. There he knelt in the sunshine and prayed to God for builders. Then he laid the first stones of the church.

Day by day the people living near came to watch him and to ask what he was building. Sometimes two or three came. Sometimes quite a crowd gathered. They watched and they talked, but they did not help.

"Who is this man?" they asked each other. Then a whisper went round that he had been a jester at the King's court.

"It's strange for a jester to build a church," they said.

"Yes, it *is* strange," replied Rahere, and he told them stories and made them laugh. But all the time he talked, he went on lifting the stones and placing them one upon another for the walls.

For a few days people came just to watch and talk. For a few more days they came to be amused, and then gradually, a few at a time, they came to help. They began to love Rahere for his fun and his gaiety, but they began to love him more for his wisdom and the kindness of his heart.

Soon nearly all the poor people of Smithfield were helping. They gave up their spare time whenever they could. The strong ones carried stones and sawed wood, and those who were not so strong passed tools, or ran errands, or came just to listen to Rahere. For Rahere was happy and bright and full of fun. He would sing or

(*Above*) Patients at St Bartholomew's Hospital enjoying the fresh air.
(*Right*) The Church of St Bartholomew the Great.

tell jokes or make up stories, and whenever he wished, he would make the people laugh—from the smallest ragged child to the cleverest of his workmen.

So at last his prayers were answered and his promise was kept, for the church and the hospital were finished. Rahere named the hospital Saint Bartholomew's, and the church Saint Bartholomew the Great.

"They are for all who need them," he said. "Anyone who asks here shall receive. Anyone who seeks shall find. And anyone who knocks may enter."

The story of Rahere belongs to the history of more than eight hundred years ago, but St Bartholomew's Hospital still cares for the sick; and the Church of St Bartholomew the Great still stands in Smithfield.

It has stood through the Fire of London, and the great wartime bombing raids. And inside, buried in a carved tomb, is the body of the man who kept his promise—Rahere, the jester who built a church.

Gold at Silver Grass

They came upon it quite suddenly—a shanty town in the hollow of the hills.

"That's strange," said Roddy. "I didn't think there was a town anywhere near Uncle Joe's ranch."

"No," agreed Mike. "Let's go and look at it anyway."

The boys steered their horses down into the valley, where a shabby store advertised candy and tobacco. Roddy tried the door, but it was locked.

"Quiet sort of place," he murmured.

They tied the horses to a post and walked on down the dusty street between rows of wooden shacks with shuttered windows and sun-blistered doors. The whole town was deadly still. Not a movement—not a sound—except the echo of their own footsteps.

"I wonder where everyone is," said Mike. He peeped through the half-open door of a dance hall. The ceiling boards sagged, and wallpaper curled dismally down to the floor. Everything looked deserted and forgotten, and a strange, uncanny silence prevailed.

"I know," remarked Roddy after a while. "It's a ghost town. People came here to mine gold and they reached the end of the gold seam, and had to give up. Look, there are mine dumps over there."

By this time they had reached a small wooden bridge, spanning the dried-up bed of a stream. Then they saw that they were not alone in the deserted town. A man stood on the bridge, gazing up at the empty houses and neglected streets. His eyes were full of dreams and regrets. Quite obviously he had known this place in happier days. He gave a start as he noticed the boys, and for him the spell was broken.

"Didn't expect to meet anyone here," he said.

"Was it a gold town?" asked Mike.

"Yes," replied the man. "Five years ago it was pulsing with people and life."

"And I suppose they came to the end of the seam," put in Roddy.

The man didn't answer. He seemed lost in his own thoughts. Then he said gruffly,

"Gold. Supposed to be the most precious thing in the world. But it isn't. There's something even more precious."

"What's that?" asked Mike.

"Water. It wasn't lack of gold that killed this town. It was lack of water." He went on talking, as much to himself as to the boys.

"I made money in gold, up at Yellow Peak, and I used it to start these Kilandy mines. I made a pretty packet here for a year or two. Then gold lost its lure for me and I became more interested in people. The men who worked the mines for me, they were good fellows. I wanted to give them decent houses to live in. I wanted to provide better conditions for their wives and children. I planned to replace the shacks with something more comfortable—to build churches and clubs and schools and parks. I dreamed of making Kilandy a model town. And just when I had made a start—the water supply failed. It's bad enough to come to the end of a gold seam and see your men out of work and your mines empty. But it's worse when you know the gold's there to be mined, and it's only water you want." He paused a moment, then added,

"I'd give anything to bring prosperity back to Kilandy."

"Jolly bad luck," agreed Roddy with sympathy;

and Mike shuffled in the dust and wished he could do something to help.

The man turned suddenly and walked swiftly up the street, as if he couldn't bear to stay in the dead town a moment longer. But he left sadness like a shadow over the bridge, so that the boys too, were filled with a desire to get away, to get away quickly.

A few minutes later, galloping back over the prairie to Silver Grass Ranch, they turned to take another look at the deserted town.

"I wish," said Roddy. "I wish—"

"So do I," muttered Mike. "I feel I'd do anything to bring prosperity back to Kilandy."

At supper time they talked to Uncle Joe about it.

"Yes," he said. "Water's a great problem in these parts. I have barely enough myself, and the well goes almost dry in the summer."

"We must go another day," put in Mike eagerly, "and take torches and explore the mines."

"There's the beginning of a mine on the ranch here," said Uncle Joe. "Someone did a bit of blasting before I took over. But he didn't get very far—not enough money, I suppose—or not enough gold to make it worth while."

"I felt so sorry for the man at Kilandy," mused Roddy. "You know, Uncle Joe—he loved Kilandy as you love your cattle—" He broke off in horror, conscious that somehow he had said the wrong thing, for Uncle Joe's face had turned pale, and he looked suddenly like an old man.

"What's the matter?" asked Mike anxiously. "Are you ill, Uncle Joe?"

"No, no. I'm all right." Uncle Joe smiled to reassure them. Then he gulped down a great mug of coffee and went on talking—a little too quickly, a little too cheerfully.

He did not, of course, deceive the boys. They knew that something was wrong. Something was very much wrong.

"Uncle," said Mike a little later. "If there's anything we can do to help, you will let us know, won't you?"

"Yes," replied Uncle Joe. Then he said slowly, "You're good lads, and I didn't want to spoil your holiday here, but I guess you'll have to know. It's the cattle—they have foot and mouth disease and it's spreading fast. It means destroying the whole herd. It's the end of everything for me. My dream was always of cattle—to build up a fine ranch—to build up a tip-top herd. It's been the work of a lifetime. And now—I guess all I can do is to sell the land for what I can get."

"Oh," murmured Roddy. "Oh, Uncle Joe, I'm so sorry." Mike said nothing, for he felt there was nothing to say. He was filled only with the deepest misery for his uncle.

After a long, unhappy silence, Roddy said haltingly,

"Couldn't you—couldn't you sell the carcases, and buy another herd!"

"Not with foot and mouth," replied Uncle Joe. "Carcases have to be burned."

He rammed tobacco into his pipe and added,

"It isn't only the money, and the loss of my living—it's the loss of fine creatures I've reared from calves. Look at Starlight. We never thought she'd live. We reared her from a most sickly calf, but today there isn't a finer beast in America. Look at Moonsplash and Cymbeline—"

His voice droned on in the fading light. He knew each beast in the herd. He kept careful records of its parentage and peculiarities, of its character and colouring. He knew every marking on its silky hide.

"Oh, it's such bad luck," thought Roddy. "It's such bad, bad luck."

The next day and the week that followed seemed endless.

"I guess the best way you can help," advised Uncle Joe kindly, "is to keep out of the way. Just amuse yourselves and keep out of the way." This the boys were eager enough to do, for all that week the killings went on, and the grey smoke of fires curled up into the sky.

Silver Grass, the ranch that had been such a sunny, happy place, had changed overnight. There were no more jokes thrown back and forth among the cowboys, no more songs drifting on the wind. The lowing of cattle ended, and the thunderous roar of the herd in motion was heard no more. A sad silence reigned. It seemed a strange, unhappy holiday for Roddy and Mike—Kilandy a ghost town—Silver Grass a dead ranch. And there was nothing they could do to help. Nothing at all.

"Let's explore the mine here," suggested Roddy one afternoon.

"All right," said Mike dully.

The boys were so sorry for Uncle Joe that they could think of nothing else, and it was therefore with no great enthusiasm that they took torches and walked over to the entrance of the mine shaft. But once they had left daylight behind them and started groping down in the darkness, they couldn't help becoming excited. Down they went in the musty dampness, flashing their torches on old mine props and walls of gold-bearing rock. This, they supposed, had been some other person's dream—some other person's plans gone wrong.

"Supposing—," said Mike slowly. "Supposing we found that this place was rich in gold; wouldn't that help Uncle Joe? He could mine gold and exchange it for a new herd of cattle, or he could sell the land for a very high price."

"No," replied Roddy, "I don't think it would help. He hasn't the money to start mining, and the old gold-rush days are over. Everyone knows that most of the land in these parts is gold-bearing. I wonder how far we are below the surface now."

"What do you think Uncle Joe will do?" mused Mike. "He'll have to get a job of some sort, but how awful it will be for him to work on a stranger's ranch after having his own all these years!"

"Mm," muttered Roddy in sympathy. The ground now became very rough and uneven, and from somewhere far away came a low, rumbling sound.

"What was that?" exclaimed Mike.

"Don't know."

The sound came again. This time it seemed nearer —a long, low rumbling.

"I don't like it," said Mike, trying to keep fear from his voice. "Let's get going. I want to get out."

"All right," replied Roddy. "Nothing to be scared

about. It's probably just an echo of some sort. All the same we'll go back if you like." He turned, touching the damp wall of rock with one hand, and reaching to help Mike with the other.

What happened next he scarcely knew. He was only aware of a noise like thunder and a great rush of falling rock. The whole earth seemed to shake, and the ground gave way beneath his feet. Desperately he clung to a mine prop, and somehow, though shaken and bruised and very insecure, he managed to keep his balance.

"Mike!" he cried. "Are you all right, Mike?"
There was no reply. There was only the noise of falling rocks, becoming fainter and fainter somewhere below. There was only the vibration of the rocky walls around.

"Mike," called Roddy in fear. "Mike! Mike! Where are you?"

The rumbling died away, and everything was quiet. Even the silence was frightening. It was worse than the eerie silence at Kilandy—worse than the tragic, unnatural silence at Silver Grass.

"Mike! Mike! Where are you?"
Roddy called and called. Then he remembered his torch. It had gone out, but a press and a shake, and it was shining again. That was a relief anyway. Not daring to move a step, he held on to the mine prop and flashed the torch around. What he saw filled him with horror.

It appeared that there had been a landslide or an earth tremor. The passage down which the boys had come still seemed to be untouched, but the passage from which they had turned back a moment ago was blocked by earth and fallen boulders. Roddy's life at least had been saved by a single step. But where was Mike?

Roddy now flashed the torch at his feet. Mike must be somewhere. But at Roddy's feet was a great hole where the ground had given way. The torch beam was not strong enough to show more than the trembling edge of it. Heaven alone knew how vast and deep it was. And down there Mike must be. He might be injured. He might be killed.

Then Roddy saw how narrow was his own margin of safety, for he stood on the very brink of the chasm. Groping beside the wall, he took a few cautious steps until he stood once more on solid ground.

Now, how to help Mike? Roddy called again and again but there was no reply. If only there were someone else who could help. If only there were ropes and lanterns. That would be the best thing perhaps—hurry up to the surface and get help—for here alone in the darkness there was little he could do.

With sickening fear for Mike, Roddy walked back along the passage, hoping that his torch would last until the end of the journey. It seemed a very long way, much longer than it had been before. On and on went

Roddy. Would it never end? The mine was no longer exciting and interesting. It was full of deep shadows and strange soft echoes.

At last a circle of daylight became visible, and Roddy in relief ran stumbling towards it. He clambered out into the fresh, clean air, and on to the yellow-green prairie land of Silver Grass Ranch. He hurried towards the house, but before he reached it, he saw Uncle Joe and two cowboys standing near the barn.

"Sorry, boys," Uncle Joe was saying. "There'll be no more work for you. I guess you'll have to pack your things and go. This is the end of Silver Grass." His face was pale with the strain and grief of the last week and his eyes were sad.

"And I've come to tell him of more trouble," thought Roddy miserably. "If only it hadn't happened *this* week."

"Uncle Joe," he panted. "We were in the old mine, and the earth gave way and Mike fell. Could you all come and bring ropes and lanterns?"

In a second Uncle Joe had put his own worries aside, and in a few minutes he and the cowboys, carrying lanterns and ropes, were hurrying beside Roddy to the mine shaft. The lanterns gave a much stronger, clearer light than the torches had done. As he trudged along in the mine again, Roddy felt vaguely surprised to see how wide the passages were. After a while an old truck came into view. Roddy remembered having seen it before.

"It's not much farther now," said he.

"Better go carefully," advised the leading cowboy. A moment later he stopped.

"I guess this is it," he said.

There it was—the scatter of boulders and the avalanche of rocks. There it was—the great hole where Mike had disappeared. Fears for Mike were forgotten for a minute while a general argument took place as to who would go down.

"Right, boys," said Uncle Joe, fastening a rope round his waist. "You can let me down below."

"You're too heavy, sir," said the leading cowboy. "I'll go."

"I'm willing to do it," put in the other.

"I guess it ought to be me," remarked Roddy. "I'm the lightest."

Uncle Joe unwillingly agreed that he himself was too heavy.

"But I don't like any of you boys risking your life," he said. "And you can't go, Roddy. That's certain."

"But he's my brother," persisted Roddy. "Besides, I weigh much less than any of you." So in the end it was Roddy who went.

"You understand?" said Uncle Joe. "Look for Mike and tie the rope round him. When you're ready to send him up, pull the rope three times. Then when he's up, we'll send it back for you."

"Yes," nodded Roddy.

They tied the rope round Roddy's waist, gave him a lantern, and let him down slowly over the edge.

"Cheerio!" said Roddy, swinging round in the

darkness. Soon he was able to steady himself a little and to assist his descent by kicking against the rocks. Down and down he went, into the very depths of the earth. He could not pretend even to himself that he was unafraid, but everything felt so strange and unreal that it seemed more like a dream than part of real life. He started whistling to give himself courage, and then to his amazement and joy, a voice came up through the blackness,

"Roddy, is that you?"

"Mike!" he exclaimed in delight. "Mike, are you all right?"

He looked down, and in a pool of lantern light he saw Mike's pale, upturned face. Next moment the boys were standing together on a pile of earth, and Roddy was slipping his arms out of the rope.

"Are you really all right?" he asked incredulously.

"A bit bruised, that's all," replied Mike. "I guess I was unconscious for a bit though. I'm glad you've come. My torch has given out."

"Better go up," said Roddy, offering the rope. "Uncle Joe and a couple of cowboys are waiting to pull you to safety."

"Wait a minute," said Mike. "I want to show you something, but don't say a word to anyone until we have Uncle Joe on his own."

Roddy looked at him in surprise. Whatever was he so

excited about, here in the depths of the earth? Probably just gold gleaming in the rocks. Mike took hold of the lantern and scrambled through a small opening, explaining that when he had first fallen, his torch had still been working.

"And look what I found!" he cried.

Roddy crawled after him and then stood up, holding the lantern high.

"What is it?" he asked, for they were standing in what appeared to be an enormous natural cave.

"Can't you see?" said Mike in delight. Then something moved in the lantern glow—a long, silver ripple creeping close to their feet.

"Water!" cried Roddy. "Water! A huge underground lake!"

"Yes," nodded Mike. "Isn't it wonderful? It might help somebody, don't you think? We'd better go back. Uncle Joe will be worried. Talk about it at supper tonight. See?"

"Yes," agreed Roddy, though he was nearly bursting with questions and ideas.

A little later he watched Mike swaying on the rope, going up and up towards safety.

That night at supper Mike recounted his adventures in detail, and told of his great discovery.

"A lake! An underground lake!" repeated Uncle Joe. "Are you sure you weren't seeing things, Mike?"

"No, really, Uncle," protested Roddy. "I saw it too. Mike showed it to me. It's enormous."

"Of course," said Uncle Joe slowly, "if it can be used, it makes the land more valuable. It means I'll get a better price for it. How I wish I'd found it twenty years ago—not that it would have helped me out of my present difficulties." He became quiet and thoughtful, and the boys chatted to each other for a while in low voices. Then Mike said,

"Uncle Joe, the lake is near enough to be piped into Kilandy, isn't it?"

"Yes, I guess it is."

"Well—that man we told you about—he'd be pleased, wouldn't he? Couldn't you sell the land to him?"

"Don't know that I like to think of pipes and workmen on land that was meant for cattle," muttered Uncle Joe.

"But water's so precious," persisted Mike. "And if you sold to him, you'd be bringing prosperity back to Kilandy, and maybe he'd pay you enough to start you up in a new ranch."

"Never be the same as Silver Grass," said Uncle Joe stubbornly.

There was a long silence. Then Mike said,

"I was thinking, you see, that if you'd offer the land to the Kilandy man, Roddy and I would go and tell him about it—save you the bother. His name's Rolf McKenna, and I know where he lives—up at Tenner's Height—a cowboy told me. We could write and ask him to meet us at Kilandy."

"Very anxious to sell my ranch for me, aren't you?" replied Uncle Joe gruffly. Then he added, "All right, old chap. Go ahead with your plans. It doesn't really

matter to me what happens to the land when I've gone. It's just that I hate the thought of anyone else having it at all."

"—And I feel," put in Roddy with shining eyes, "I feel, Uncle Joe, that if prosperity returns to Kilandy, somehow prosperity will return to you too."

Uncle Joe was too depressed to believe in such a turn in fortune. All the same he couldn't help feeling cheered a little by the discovery of the lake and by the excitement of the boys.

So one morning a few days later Roddy and Mike galloped once more towards Kilandy. There it was, nestling in the hollow of the hills, but this time the sun was gleaming on roof tops, and the sky above was a vivid blue.

"Sun's shining," remarked Roddy. "It wasn't

before."

Once more they passed the closed candy shop, and tied their horses to a post. Once more they walked down the dusty street, shattering the silence with the echo of their footsteps. But this time specks of sunshine glinted through the shutters, and the ghost town seemed to be waiting—waiting to be called to life.

And there on the bridge in the appointed place was Rolf McKenna, staring as before at the neglected streets.

"Well, boys," he said, "it was a mysterious letter you sent me. I hope you haven't brought me all this way for nothing."

"Oh, no," they assured him.

"Well, what is it that's so important that it can't be trusted by letter?"

"It's about Kilandy," began Roddy. "You said you'd do anything to bring prosperity back to Kilandy, and we felt the same way about it. You said it was water you wanted. Well, we've found you the water—" Here Mike took up the tale.

He spoke about Silver Grass Ranch, and Uncle Joe's loss of his herd. He spoke of the old mine shaft and his own discovery of the underground lake.

"It isn't very far from here," he said, "and we thought you might be interested."

"Interested!" repeated Rolf McKenna. He certainly was interested, but he was cautious too, and not quite willing to believe that things were as good as they sounded.

"Well, boys," he said at last, "it's very kind of you to come and tell me all this. Now supposing I came back to Silver Grass Ranch with you, do you think your uncle would put me up for the night?"

"Oh, yes."

"You see, naturally I want to go down the mine myself. Have you plenty of ropes and lanterns? And are there any men to let me down the hole you mentioned?"

"Oh, yes, the cowboys are there at least till the end of the week."

"Right—you lead me home."

If Uncle Joe felt sick with envy at the sight of the

stranger who might buy Silver Grass, he certainly hid his feelings, for he was as hospitable and kind as ever, and he arranged at once for Rolf McKenna to explore the mine.

"I'll come with you," he said, "and the cowboys too—but if you don't mind, we'll leave Roddy and Mike above ground. We don't want them falling down any more holes and discovering lakes." The boys grinned, and to Uncle Joe's surprise didn't even argue. Maybe they preferred to be above ground.

The day seemed very long to them. The men stayed below surface most of the afternoon, and when they came up, Uncle Joe and Rolf McKenna rode over the ranch to the west. Then when it grew dark, they shut themselves up in Uncle Joe's study and talked and talked.

"I wish they'd hurry up and let us know what they think about the lake," remarked Mike.

"Perhaps it's not deep enough to be any good," suggested Roddy.

"Or perhaps Uncle Joe refuses to sell at McKenna's price."

The boys even had supper on their own, but when it was over, Uncle Joe came in with a tray of boiling coffee and mugs for four.

"Now, boys," he said. "We'll let Rolf do the talking shall we?"

Rolf McKenna followed him and sank slowly into an armchair.

"Roddy," he began, "Mike, I can never thank you enough. You've made a wonderful discovery! Not only is it a fine large lake, but it's fed by a natural, underground spring, and I'm certain it can be piped into Kilandy. The first time I met you I told you that water was more precious than gold, didn't I? Well, gold fetches a high price, so I'm willing to pay a higher price for water. But I've been explaining to your uncle, I don't really want to buy his land. I only want access to the lake and the right to lay a pipe line from Silver Grass to Kilandy. So he can keep the ranch for his new herd. I'll pay for the water supply, and I'll pay in cattle—the

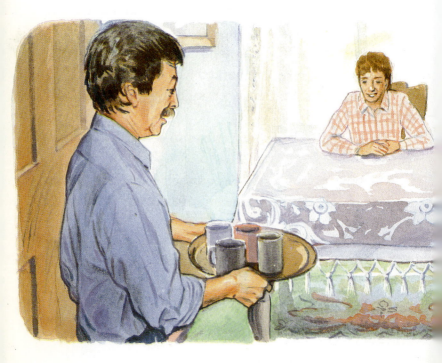

finest cattle in all America. How many did you say you had in your old herd, Joe?"

He paused, and the boys looked at him with shining eyes.

"You mean—" said Roddy. "You mean you'll give Uncle Joe a whole new herd in exchange for this lake?"

"I mean just that," replied Rolf. "It's worth it to me."

"Oh, Uncle Joe!" whispered Mike, and he was so pleased that he could think of nothing else to say. But Roddy leapt up with a cry of wild and joyous excitement.

"Prosperity returns to Kilandy!" he yelled. "Prosperity returns to Silver Grass! Oh, Mike, pour me out some coffee quickly. I'm dying of thirst."

Kek Attacks

Kek stood outside the wattle hut and stretched himself in the sunset. The wind ruffled his shaggy hair and tugged at the animal skin that clothed him.

"Ha!" said Kek aloud, for he (a boy of Ancient Britain) was growing tall and strong, and he was feeling proud of himself and glad to be alive.

It was then that he saw the Roman legions pass. He had heard many stories about the Romans—how they had come in ships, how they had fought with swords and conquered much of the country. But it was the

first time they had come this way, and Kek now hid behind the hut and trembled.

The Roman legions—he saw the glint of their armour through the trees, and the flash of their shields in the shade. He heard the rhythmic beat of their marching feet and the rattle of their swords at their sides. They looked fine and strong, the Roman legions. Kek stared at them, fascinated by the glory of their attire, and in his heart there smouldered and grew strong a fierce and burning hate.

At that moment his elder brother Bala slipped through the trees and stood silently beside him. Bala waited until the last Roman had passed. Then he said angrily, "They've come to take our land. We'll never give it up to them."

"Never," repeated Kek bravely. "We'll fight them. We'll kill them."

Other people appeared from huts and woods and stood talking in hushed voices. They all spoke of the Roman enemy—some in fear, but most of them in anger and indignation.

"We'll fight," was the general cry. "And we'll not cease from fighting until every Roman is driven back into the sea."

Early next morning the tribe began its preparations for battle. Knives, arrows and javelins were sharpened; slings and stones were made ready. Horses were fed and harnessed, and creaking chariots were cleaned.

Then on the day that followed, the warriors rode away to attack the Roman camp beyond the hill. Kek and Bala and other boys who lived near watched them go. Then they divided themselves into Romans and Britons, and began a mock battle of their own. It was always Bala's side that won, for not only was Bala older than the others, but he was a skilled fighter—better even than many men.

"If Bala could join the army," laughed the boys, "then surely the Romans would soon be beaten."

In the afternoon one of the warriors came riding home. He looked hot and weary, and he had ridden so fast that he had scarcely breath enough to speak. The boys and their families clustered round him.

"How goes the battle?" they asked.

"We're outnumbered," panted the warrior. "I've come for more men—anyone who can throw a javelin or shoot an arrow."

There was a buzz of excitement, and no lack of volunteers. All the men except the very old were ready to go.

"Bala," said someone, "you're a good fighter—and nearly a man. You had better come too!"

So Bala said goodbye and joined the new makeshift army.

"Bala will soon defeat the Romans," said Kek with a smile. "Come back quickly, Bala, won't you?" He looked at his brother in envy and admiration, and watched him ride over the hill.

But two days later when the soldiers returned, weary and defeated, half their number was missing. Some men had been killed, some wounded and some taken prisoner.

Eagerly Kek ran among them looking for Bala. Bala was not there.

"He isn't killed?" whispered Kek in fear. "He can't be killed."

"No," replied a neighbouring soldier. "Bala has been taken prisoner."

"Oh!" Kek could hardly believe—didn't want to believe—the bad news, and in the weeks that followed he watched and waited for his brother. He gazed continually at the hill, expecting to see him coming home safely after all, but Bala did not come.

Weeks and months passed. The Roman camp grew into a town, with wide streets and great buildings of stone. Some of the Britons began to mingle with the enemies, talking to them, even working for them. Kek sometimes wandered through the town, hoping to catch a glimpse of Bala. He stared in wonder at the mighty buildings. He even crept through unguarded doors, but there was never any sign of his brother, and Kek's hatred of the Romans grew ever stronger.

Bala meanwhile was receiving fairly good treatment, for the Romans had soon discovered his skill at fighting, and they had decided to train him as a gladiator, to fight in the arena when they wanted entertainment. So he travelled to different parts of the country where the Romans had already settled. He learnt to speak their language and to use their swords, and on holidays and festivals he fought other gladiators in the open-air theatres. He was not unhappy, but he often thought of

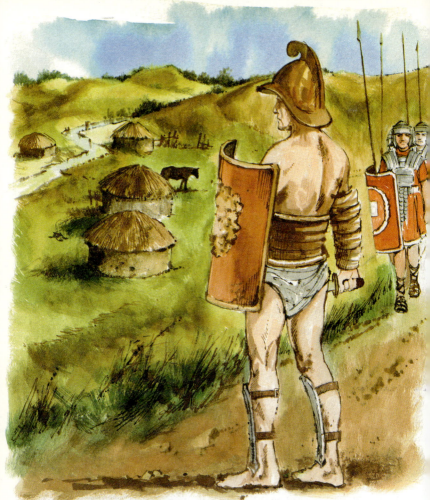

his own people, and he longed and longed to see Kek. Two years passed.

Then at last, as Bala was travelling north with the army one day, he suddenly saw scenery that he knew—a hill rising in the distance, and low trees and winding streams in the valley. There were the patches of golden corn and the scattered wattle huts—and there, small and far away, were the shaggy-haired, wild-looking people of his own tribe. His heart beat fast with excitement. This was his own land. This was home!

Where before the Roman camp had been, Bala now saw a flourishing town, and where, long ago, he and Kek had played, there was now a huge arena. The grass had been worn smooth by Roman feet, and there were tiers of seats in a complete circle.

"You'll be fighting there in a few days," a Roman soldier remarked. "The Emperor is coming. There will be a holiday and a great entertainment."

"Whom shall I fight?" asked Bala.

"Lions maybe," was the reply, but Bala smiled. He knew he was too useful to the Romans to be wasted on lions. Then he sighed and looked across the valley. There, somewhere there, was little brother Kek. Oh, if only he could see him!

Now it happened that, just at that time, Kek's hatred of the Romans moved him at last to action. He was standing with a group of friends, when some Roman soldiers came along, carrying scythes.

"Here," said one roughly to the boys. "Cut the corn for us." He pointed to a field of corn, golden and ready for reaping. The boys stepped back, clutching their home-made javelins. Cut the corn—their own fathers' corn—and give it to the Romans? No, indeed! They shook their shaggy heads and disappeared like streaks of lightning among the trees.

The afternoon wore on—hot and sultry. Slowly the boys crept back to see who had consented to cut the corn. To their surprise they saw four Roman soldiers bending low in the field, swinging scythes among the golden stems.

"Ha!" whispered Kek with pleasure. "They're having to cut it themselves!"

"Look," said a boy called Yill. "They've taken off their armour. It lies on the path."

"How dare they take our corn!" muttered Stine. Kek looked at his friends with wide, fierce eyes.

"The Romans are undefended," he said. "Who is brave enough to attack them? Who will come with me?"

"I," whispered Yill.

"I," whispered Stine.

"I," whispered the others.

"All right." Kek lay down on the ground and dragged himself slowly through the corn. The other boys followed. Slowly, slowly they advanced. Slowly, slowly they drew nearer to the unsuspecting soldiers.

Then suddenly, with a loud, wild battle cry, Kek leapt to his feet and hurled his javelin through the air. Yill repeated the cry more loudly, more wildly, and in a flash six angry, reckless British boys had thrown themselves upon the enemy.

Taken by surprise, the Roman soldiers were for a moment at a disadvantage. Then they laughed at the boldness of the young creatures before them; and the boys, before they could recover from the counter-attack, found themselves being dragged away to the Roman town.

"Let us go! Let us go!" yelled Stine.

"We will *kill* you," roared Kek.

"Big words from small boys," said the soldiers scornfully. "We'll see what you have to say to the Emperor."

Struggling and fighting all the way, the boys were taken to a stone building where they were imprisoned.

Kek was filled with misery and bitterness. He had meant to save the corn from the Romans, and all he had done had been to lead his best friends into danger—perhaps into death. Darkness was falling and the boys curled up together on the floor and slept and woke through the long night. Though they longed for morning, they also dreaded it, for they guessed that in the morning their fate would be decided.

★ ★ ★ ★ ★ ★

Next day the door was unlocked and a Roman guard entered.

"This afternoon," he said, "there's to be a great entertainment in the amphitheatre, and one of the items will be a fight between a gladiator and a prisoner. The prisoner will be one of you, and if the prisoner loses, then you'll all remain here in the town as slaves, but if he wins, you'll be set free. Now which of you will fight for the others?" No one spoke, but every boy glanced at Kek. He was the best fighter among them. Kek swallowed hard. He had led his friends into danger. It was now his task to free them—if he could.

"I will fight the gladiator," he said.

So in the afternoon he was taken to the amphitheatre and given a shield and a sword. He looked at the great circular stretch of smooth grass and at the green banks bordering it. He looked at the Roman soldiers. There were hundreds of them—sitting in rows, waiting for the next part of the holiday entertainment. Already they had witnessed cock-fighting, and bull-baiting. Now they were to see a British prisoner trying his strength against a Roman gladiator. They leaned forward eagerly. This should be interesting.

Kek was shown into the arena, and at the same moment the gladiator appeared at the opposite side. The gladiator was tall and powerful. His sword flashed, and his curved helmet glinted in the sun.

Kek gave a gasp of horror. He—a young boy— was to fight this full-grown man, this trained gladiator. It wasn't a fair contest. How could he possibly hope to win? He was facing certain death!

Then he remembered his friends—waiting—hoping—depending on him to give them freedom. He *must* win! Somehow he *must* win!

Bravely he raised the clumsy sword, and with a loud, fierce battle cry he rushed to the attack. Then he paused, amazed, for the gladiator stepped aside saying softly,

"Don't strike me, Kek!" And the gladiator dropped his own sword and held out both hands in welcome. Kek was puzzled. The gladiator had a British voice, and

there was something strangely familiar about him. Could it be—? Could it possibly be—?

"Bala!" cried Kek. "Is it you?"

"Yes," was the reply. "It's Bala."

The Romans in the audience looked at each other in surprise. This was a strange fight—where a gladiator threw down his sword and embraced his opponent! An officer jumped down into the arena.

"Fight!" he ordered. "The Emperor commands you to fight."

But Bala held his head high and answered,

"Tell the Emperor that I have fought in Roman arenas for two years, but I can't fight today—for this young British boy, who was prepared to fight so bravely, is my brother."

"Fight," said the soldier softly, "It's more than your life is worth to disobey."

"No," replied Bala. "I won't fight my brother."

There was a horrified silence as the soldier returned to the Emperor. Only Kek dared to speak, whispering to Bala about Yill and Stine and the other boys. A moment passed. Then the soldier walked back to the arena and summoned Kek and Bala to the Emperor. This might mean death for both of them.

"I understand," said the Emperor to Bala, "that you have fought in Roman arenas for two years, but that you have refused to obey my command to fight today."

"Yes," replied Bala.

"It takes courage to fight," went on the Emperor thoughtfully, "but on such an occasion as this it must take more courage to refuse to fight."

Bala nodded, for indeed it was true.

"You are brave boys," said the Emperor, "and though you belong to a conquered race, I cannot but admire you. You need not fight. Instead, as this is a Roman holiday, I will grant you one request each."

"Oh!" Bala's eyes shone. "I beseech you, mighty Caesar, to grant freedom to my brother Kek and the boys who were imprisoned with him."

The Emperor nodded consent, then glanced inquiringly at Kek.

"And I—" panted Kek, "I ask for the freedom of this my brother, Bala."

★ ★ ★ ★ ★ ★

That evening seven boys walked over the hill towards home. There in the valley were the wattle huts and the winding streams. There were the low, green trees and the patches of golden corn.

"Home!" cried Bala happily, and Yill and Stine danced beside him for joy. But Kek was deep in thought.

"A conquered race," he murmured. "Conquered —yet unconquerable."

Les Pauvres Petits

Lola sprawled on the dusty ground reading a tattered magazine she had found in the street. Marco sat beside her, frowning at his own bitter thoughts.

This was Italy. This was home—but what a home!

The city, once beautiful, was now in two distinct parts. In the north there were towers and spires and houses and shops; and life went on as usual in the busy streets. But in the south the war had left desolation and destruction. Scarcely a house remained standing. There were only broken walls and burnt-out rooms and piles of bricks and rubble. It was like a ghost town.

And among the ruins lived the children who had lost homes and parents. Like a ragged, youthful army, they darted in and out among the shadows, snatching food where they could find it, and growing thinner and paler and dirtier week by week.

Marco and Lola had lost everything. Their home had been bombed to the ground, and their parents killed. There was no one to help them or give them shelter, and for several months now they had fended for themselves like hungry animals. The war was over, but peace made no difference to their hard and cheerless lives.

"I'm going out with the gang tonight," said Marco suddenly. Lola looked up from her magazine, and her dark eyes filled with horror.

"Oh, Marco!" she cried. "You know what the gang children do—they steal from shops and cafés. You've always said you wouldn't do it—" Marco shrugged his shoulders.

"We're hungry," he replied. "I *must* do it."

"But stealing—," wailed Lola.

"When your way of living changes, your ideas have to change," he said, using the same arguments that the other boys had used with him. "Rudolfo says that if our lives have been spared, it's our duty to keep ourselves healthy. If we don't eat, we'll die. I'll steal only a little food, Lola—just enough for our needs."

"But you might get caught by the police—" began Lola. Then she stopped. It was no good. She had known that this would have to happen soon. Marco had made up his mind, and when he was so hungry, who could blame him?

And Marco of course didn't tell her that what had finally decided him, had not been his own hunger, but Stefano's scornful remark.

"Well, if I had a sister who looked as starved and ill as Lola, *I* shouldn't be afraid to steal for her."

Later that afternoon Rudolfo and Stefano suddenly

appeared. They were walking cautiously, looking to right and left as if fearful of being followed.

"We're not going tonight after all," said Stefano softly.

"Why not?" asked Marco.

"Tito has heard that the police are on the warpath. They are trying to round up all gang children and put them in a Home."

"A Home?" repeated Lola. "Surely that would be a good thing?"

"Lola!" cried Rudolfo in disgust. "Would you want to give up your freedom and have all your curls cut off— and cooped up in a great bare building—and not allowed out, and—"

"Never," interrupted Marco with determination. "We'll never, never, never set foot in a Children's Home."

Lola left the boys talking, and went back to her book. Anyway a Home would be clean, she thought—for she longed to be clean again.

After a while when Stefano and Rudolfo had crept away as cautiously as they had come, Marco looked enviously at his sister and said,

"I wish you'd hurry up and finish that magazine, so that I could read it."

"You might find another if you look," she murmured.

"So I might," thought Marco, and he began searching in a pile of rubble. Slowly he burrowed his hands into it, putting aside bits of brick and plaster, scraps of metal and wood. Then he found a teddy bear's arm.

"This looks hopeful," he said, and he went on searching.

Suddenly he saw a scrap of paper with printing on it. Ah! A torn page! He dug his hands deeply into the pile again. More pieces of paper came away in his fingers. Not books—not pages—but bank notes—money! Marco gasped. Money!

"Lola! Lola! Look!" he called.

Lola dropped her magazine and ran to her brother. She too delved into the rubble and pulled out money.

"Oh, isn't it lovely—lovely?" she cried, her eyes shining with joy. "We'll be able to buy food for all the others."

"Supper tonight for the whole gang," added Marco, "—and a pair of shoes for you."

"Oh, yes, yes!"

The children were wildly excited. Nothing like this had ever happened before. They were lucky! They were lucky!

Then Marco grew suddenly quiet, and started putting the notes together and bundling them into his pockets.

"Lola," he said, "if we buy food for the gang, the money will all be gone in less than a week. Then we

shall all be hungry again. Let's buy railway tickets and go to Grandmother in France."

Lola sat back on her heels and nodded her head vigorously. This was the answer to all their troubles.

"Let's go to the station at once," she said.

There was nothing to pack, nothing to take except the bundle of notes and the tattered magazine. Gaily the children ran down the streets, dodging through the ruins, jumping over loose bricks, until at last they reached the station.

Then just as they were walking towards the ticket office, Lola stood still and said in the hesitant way that Marco knew so well,

"Marco—do you think—?"

"Oh, Lola," he said impatiently, "you're going to say the money isn't really ours, and we ought not to use it. What about Father's money in our own house? That might be found one day. It might be found by children like us—who need it. We needed money and it has been sent to us. We should be grateful." He gave his sister no more chance to argue, but hurried forward to the ticket window and put down the bundle of notes.

A moment later he was showing Lola the precious tickets to France, and saying, "We still have lots of money left, and the train doesn't leave till eleven tonight. Let's have a meal and then go back to the town and give the rest of the money to Rudolfo."

It was only when they were seated in the train several hours later that Marco and Lola remembered the shoes they had meant to buy.

"Never mind," said Marco. "We'll be at Grandmother's tomorrow, and then everything will be all right." They both clutched bags of food and some books from the bookstall, and they both thought of Rudolfo and Stefano's joy at the unexpected present of money—enough to buy rolls and coffee for the whole gang.

Then their thoughts turned again to Grandmother. It was a long time since they had visited her in France, but they had happy memories of her kindness and affection and of her pleasant little house near the English Channel. She would be sad to hear about Mother and Father of course, but she would be surprised and delighted to see the children. They would be clean and warm and well fed again. They would have clothes and books and a home. They would be happy in France with Grandmother.

The journey was long, but Marco and Lola enjoyed it. In a carriage full of friendly people they found themselves telling their story. Everyone made a great fuss of them, and as the train jogged on through the night, they leaned comfortably against their fellow travellers and fell asleep.

The next afternoon they arrived at the coastal town where Grandmother lived.

"Rue de la Dalle," murmured Marco. "I wonder where it is?"

Tired but very happy, they hurried along the streets, chattering in French to each other in readiness for talking to Grandmother.

"There it is! There it is!" cried Lola. There was the Rue de la Dalle. There was Grandmother's house just as they remembered it. Eagerly they knocked on the door. Eagerly they waited. There were footsteps. In a moment—in just a moment Grandmother would come —and then everything would be all right.

The door opened. A woman stood framed in the sunlight. It was not Grandmother.

"Grand'mere?" queried Marco. "Madame Marcelle?"

"Madame Marcelle is dead," said the woman kindly. "She died six weeks ago. She was very old, you know."

"Oh!" whispered Marco.

The woman looked curiously at the two ragged, handsome children.

"Are you the Italian grandchildren?" she asked.

"Yes," answered Marco in a choking voice. "Our house was bombed and our parents were killed. We came to France to live with Grandmother."

"Les pauvres petits," crooned the woman, whose name was Madame Henri. "You poor little children. Come in and rest, and tell me all about yourselves. You are tired, I expect, and hungry. I'll make you coffee. It isn't very good coffee, but it's the best we can buy."

She gathered the children in her arms and ushered them into the house. She gave them coffee and cake, and she called the neighbours in to see them.

"The Italian grandchildren of Madame Marcelle," she said. "Les pauvres petits! All this way they have come, and their grandmother is dead."

The neighbours swarmed in and listened to the children's halting French. They all said, "Poor little things," a hundred times, and "Terrible! Terrible!" a hundred more. They all fussed and murmured and shed tears of sympathy, until Marco and Lola, who had been brave for so long, broke down and wept. They put their arms on the table, and their heads in their arms, and nothing would comfort them.

That night, for the first time in months, they had hot baths and a good supper. Madame Henri tucked them up in her own bed. She kissed them a dozen times with murmurs of "Poor little things", and "Goodnight".

Then she went to satisfy the needs of her own large family and to make a bed for herself on the floor. And Marco and Lola, clean and comfortable at last, forgot their troubles for a while, and slept.

For five days after that everything went smoothly. Madame Henri was loving and motherly, and though she had neither food nor money to spare, she went without things herself in order to feed her visitors. One of the neighbours produced clothes that her own children had outgrown—shorts and a jacket for Marco, and sandals and a frock for Lola. All the people in the Rue de la Dalle were as kind and helpful as they could possibly be. Marco and Lola began to feel that life was not so bad after all. Then came the next blow.

They were sitting on a couch, laughing and trying to read a French story book, when they became aware of Madame Henri's voice in the kitchen. She always talked rather loudly and she usually talked a great deal, so at first the children didn't take any notice. Then suddenly they realised that she was talking about them.

"Les pauvres petits," she was saying to a neighbour, "poor little things, I'd love to keep them of course, but you know what it is—I just haven't the room—and with prices what they are today and my own family growing so fast, I simply can't afford to take on two extra—"

"No, of course not," agreed the neighbour.

"However," continued Madame Henri, "I've been to see the police, and they've arranged for them to go into the Children's Home. Someone's coming to fetch them tomorrow afternoon at four o'clock. Poor things, they won't want to go—but they'll get used to it—"

Get used to it! Marco and Lola looked at each other in horror, and their blood ran cold.

"Never!" whispered Marco. "We'll never go into a Children's Home—never, never, never!"

"We were foolish to imagine that Madame Henri would keep us for ever," murmured Lola. "Of course she can't afford it, and she hasn't even a bed for herself while we are here."

"We'll run away," said Marco.

So they made plans. They decided that they would go out immediately after lunch the next day. They would leave a note for Madame Henri, and they would never come back.

But their plans didn't work, for next morning about eleven o'clock there was a knock at the door. It came just as Madame Henri was preparing herself to tell the children about the Home. Indeed she had actually started saying.

"Mes pauvres petits—my poor little ones—there is something I must tell you—," but she broke off abruptly and went to answer the door. There she found a policeman and a lady from the Home.

"This afternoon—you said this afternoon—" began Madame Henri.

"Yes," said the policeman. "We apologise if we have upset your plans; but if the children are in, it will be more convenient if this lady can take them now. As for me—I wish to have a few particulars from them first."

"Oh, dear, oh, dear!" wailed Madame Henri. "Les pauvres petits. I haven't broken the news to them yet. Come in. Come in. Poor little ones, they won't want to go. Perhaps I could come with you to see that they are comfortable."

"Certainly, certainly," was the reply, and everyone trooped into the sitting-room, expecting to see the

children. But there was no one there.

"Marco! Lola!" called Madame Henri. Then she turned to the lady and policeman, and her hands fluttered like flying birds as she wailed,

"Oh, dear, they must have heard your voices. They have gone—gone—the poor little things!"

The policeman moved to the front door and the others followed. They were just in time to see two frightened children dash round the corner of the road and out of sight.

"Quick! Quick!" panted Marco to Lola. "They've seen us! They're coming!"

From street to street ran the children—along the highways and byways of the French town—and behind them came the policeman and the Home lady and Madame Henri, who still had enough breath to murmur "Poor little things" every few seconds.

A sudden narrow turning brought the children unexpectedly to the harbour, where a British troopship was preparing to depart. Marco scrambled through a fence, and Lola followed. On the quay lay a pile of kit-bags. Quick as lightning each child crept into one, crouched down, and was quite still.

They waited. For a few moments nothing happened. Then they felt themselves being swung aloft and dumped down heavily.

They must be on the ship. The ship was probably going to England. Madame Henri would never find them there.

Marco was fortunate. Still hidden in the kit-bag, he was taken to a cabin and left on the floor. Lola was not so lucky. A soldier glanced at her kit-bag and muttered,

"Doesn't look like mine. My name's on it though." He plunged his hand through the opening and touched something which certainly did not belong to him. Lola, crouching in terror, felt his fingers tangled in her hair—so she could do nothing other than rise into view like a mermaid coming out of the sea.

"Well!" exclaimed the soldier. Lola knew not a word of English, and she felt it was useless to try explaining in Italian or French. So she raised her sad, dark eyes appealingly and said nothing.

"Sorry, honey," said the soldier. "I'd love to keep you, but I don't *think* the colonel would approve." He helped her out of the kit-bag, and led her firmly down the gangway and on to the quay.

Meanwhile Marco was intolerably hot. He wondered if Lola were anywhere near him. Ah! the ship was moving. Cautiously he raised his head and listened. There seemed to be no one about. He peeped out and found that he was in a cabin. He had a great desire to take a last look at France, so he climbed out of the bag and went to the porthole. He stood on tiptoe and gazed at the quay.

Oh! Horror gripped his heart. He saw Lola, sitting on a box, staring at the ship. Her hair hung in a glorious mass of tangled, black curls, and beside her stood the policeman, and the lady and Madame Henri. Lola didn't struggle or try to escape. She didn't even cry. She only stared at the ship in utter, utter despair.

"Oh!" cried Marco, and at that moment the ship swung round, and France was hidden from sight. There was only a view of the wide grey sea stretching away and away into the distance, like the unknown future.

Marco sat down on the edge of a bunk and sobbed. It didn't matter what happened to him now. He just didn't care.

A little later an officer came into the cabin. He glanced at his luggage lying on the floor, and thought, "Good! That's arrived safely." Then he saw Marco, who was still sitting on the edge of the bunk in the depths of misery.

"What's the trouble?" asked the soldier kindly.

Marco only gulped and went on crying.

"Of course," thought the soldier, "he's a foreigner—looks French," so he repeated in French, "What's the trouble?"

"My sister," wailed Marco in his own language. "My sister—she's left on the quay. They'll put her in a Home—she's all alone—"

"Italian?" said the soldier. "Now if you speak very slowly, I'll be able to understand you. Tell me all about it."

There was no mistaking the kindness in his voice,

even though his Italian was a little strange. So Marco told him about his home in Italy, and then about the bombing. He told how he and Lola had lived in streets and alleys, searching even in dustbins to find scraps of food. He told about Rudolfo and the gang children, and about finding the money, and travelling to Grandmother's house. He told about Madame Henri and how she had planned to put them in a Home. He told about the chase through the town, and how he and Lola had hidden in kit-bags. And last of all he told how he had looked out of the porthole and seen Lola sitting on the quay in France.

The soldier listened in silence, except for an occasional reminder of,

"Slowly. Slowly."

Then he took a deep breath, and muttered,

"Poor kid! You poor kid!"

Marco rubbed his eyes, and looked up and asked,

"What can I do? What can I do?"

"Listen," said the soldier in his kind, strange Italian. "I'm being demobbed. I'm going home to my wife in England. Come and stay with us for a while. We'll find out about your sister. We can write to Madame Henri. She'll be able to tell us about Lola, won't she? You stay here while I go and see the commanding officer and the ship's captain. You're really a stowaway, you see—but don't worry. I'll fix everything for you."

He gave Marco a pat of encouragement, and swung out of the cabin. He was away a long time—so long that Marco began to be afraid that he was not managing to fix things after all. Then suddenly he came back.

"That's fine," he said. "Everything's fine." He sat down on the bunk beside Marco and added,

"You can call me Philip. And instead of worrying about your sister, supposing you try to learn a little English. Say—'Good morning, Philip,' for a start."

Marco tried twisting his tongue round the new words. Italian was a fine language, and French was not bad, but English was very strange.

"Good morning, Philip," he said slowly. Then he laughed because it sounded so funny.

For months after that, Marco felt that he must be dreaming. He lived now in a beautiful house on the edge of the Sussex Downs. Philip and his wife Angela were kind and jolly. Marco went to school and made friends with English boys. He was never hungry, never cold. He was comfortable and happy, and life was so easy that he half expected to awake and find himself back in the bombed buildings where he and Lola had lived for so long.

Lola! It was only the thought of Lola that worried him. She wrote to him often. She lived in the Children's Home in France.

"I'm quite happy," wrote Lola in her letters, "only

there's no one to speak Italian to me, and I miss you very much."

One day Philip suggested that she should come to England for the summer holiday.

"You understand," he explained to Marco, "we'd like to give her a home here, for your sake, but we really can't have you both, so we'll let her stay just for the holiday. Then she'll have to go back to France."

"Yes," said Marco. "You're very kind." But to himself he added hopefully,

"Perhaps when they *see* Lola—perhaps when they *see* her—"

Then at last one afternoon Lola arrived. During the first evening, after the excitement of meeting Marco, she was very quiet. She sat on the edge of an armchair and gazed dreamily at everything in the room. Philip and Angela looked at her sad, dark eyes and her mass of black curls and wondered what she was thinking.

Suddenly she stood up and spread out her hands, and said in Italian,

"Marco—our own home in Italy—it was quite different from this—but somehow it *felt* the same, didn't it?"

She spoke so slowly that even Angela understood, and Angela looked across at Philip with a question in her eyes.

Philip nodded, and said gruffly,

"Marco, ask Lola if she'd like to stay here for good."

"For ever?" murmured Marco, hardly daring to believe it.

"Yes, we'll manage somehow."

Marco put his arm round Lola and broke into a torrent of excited Italian. Then he turned to Philip and Angela and cried,

"She says, 'Yes—yes—yes, *please*'." And he repeated it in Italian, French and English, so that there should be no mistake.

A Cinderella

When Robert Louis Stevenson died in Samoa, his wife, who was American, made plans to return to her homeland. Before she set sail she heard the sad story of a little orphan girl, born of a Samoan mother and an American father. At the age of five, she had been sent to school in San Francisco. Her father had left money and lands to her in Samoa, but she seemed to have no one to help her to claim them. Other people were using the land, or receiving the rent for it. No one remained in touch with the child, and no one even knew the name of the school where she was supposed to be.

Mrs Stevenson decided to try and trace her and help her, as she herself was intending to live in San Francisco. As soon as she settled there, she began to make inquiries at local boarding schools, but none of them had heard of the little girl.

At last she tracked down a child with a similar name, not at a school, but at an orphanage. She received permission to see her, and she went to the orphanage, taking a Samoan basket and some shells. We don't know how old the little girl was by then, but she was certainly not old enough to understand her bewildering situation, so far away from home.

She didn't know why this lady had come to visit her, but she at once recognised the Samoan basket as

Mrs Robert Louis Stevenson

something from home. She ran forward with a cry of delight, and she put her hand in among the cold, familiar shells.

Kind Mrs Stevenson now set out to prove the child's claim to the lands and money. This wasn't easy, and she travelled the long distance to Washington, where she sought the help of senators, priests and lawyers, and at last met with success.

The little girl was declared the rightful owner of the lands, and some of the back rent was restored to her. She had relatives in Samoa who were anxious to look after her, so Mrs Stevenson took her away from the orphanage. She took her into her own home for a while. She bought new clothes for her, and gave a party for her. Then she put her on a ship to Samoa, and waved her off to a happier life.

A Bargain

Darkness covered Diamond Grove and merged with the shadows of the Ozark Hills. The village was hushed, and farms and plantations stretched away into the distance in sleeping silence.

On Farmer Carver's land all was peaceful. He and his wife were asleep in the farmhouse, and Mary, the black slave, lay with her sick baby in the log cabin across the yard.

But out of the stillness came the sound of horses' hooves, galloping, galloping across the hills; and out of the stillness came the sound of muffled footsteps and whispered voices. The nightriders were out! They were out to steal—not horses, not cattle, but slaves; for though the days of slavery in America were drawing to

an end, there were still good prices to be paid for strong slaves bought and sold in the markets.

So, suddenly Farmer Carver was awakened by a scream, and by the time he had scrambled out of bed and reached the log cabin, it was empty. Mary, the gentle black woman who helped in the house, had gone; and gone too was her small, sick child.

"Mary!" cried Mrs Carver, rushing to the door in alarm. "We must get Mary back."

"I'll follow them," said the farmer, and slipping on a coat he ran to the stable for his horse. It was a fine horse —stronger, faster probably than any horse the nightriders rode. In a moment Farmer Carver had mounted it and was speeding away towards the village.

Diamond Grove was in a state of uproar, for the thieves had been there too, and many people had discovered the loss of their slaves.

"Some of us must follow!" cried a man. "Who will come?" There was no lack of volunteers. Quickly villagers brought out their horses and prepared to depart.

"Look here," said Farmer Carver to a friend. "I don't like leaving my wife alone out there. If I go back, will you try to get our slave Mary for us?"

The man nodded readily.

"They'll ask a price," he said.

"Of course, I'll give you the money," replied the farmer, but even as he said it, he realised that he had none with him.

"Oh!" he muttered impatiently. "Give them something. Take my horse. Give them that if you must, but get Mary and the baby back somehow."

"Right!" The group of horsemen were off in the darkness, and Farmer Carver returned home in a borrowed cart. It was a fine horse. He hoped the man would not have to sacrifice it—but Mary was a good slave, and his wife was fond of her. Perhaps it would be worth giving up the horse to get Mary back.

Days passed, days of wondering uncertainty and continual anxiety. Mrs Carver grew quite ill with worry, and the farmer's face was grim as he wandered over the farm without his precious horse.

Meanwhile the village men, after losing the track for some time, came quite suddenly upon the thieves. They were afraid to fire upon them in case the slaves should get hurt, but they managed to make a shouted bargain, offering to give Farmer Carver's horse for Mary and the baby.

"Agreed," said the nightriders. "Tie the horse to a tree, and retreat six hundred paces. When you hear our horn, return to the tree, and there you will find the slave and the baby."

The men tied up the horse and retreated along the bend of the river. Rain was falling and the sky was black with a growing storm. They did not trust the nightriders, but this was their only chance of saving Mary, and they felt they must take it. They waited some time, and when at last the sound of the horn broke into their angry thoughts, it came from far away, and they knew that the nightriders had made their escape.

They went forward to the tree. The horse had gone, and there in the rain lay a dirty, wet, cold bundle—the tiny, shivering baby. Of Mary, the mother, there was no sign. The nightriders had tricked them. The nightriders had ridden away into the distance.

A few days later the men returned to Diamond Grove and two of them rode out to Farmer Carver's farm and told their story.

"You exchanged my horse for *this*!" exclaimed the

farmer. "You gave my valuable horse for this poor, sick babe! What a bargain!"

But Mrs Carver took the wet, shivering bundle and changed the dirty wrappings. The baby appeared to be dead, but with loving care, she gave it warmth and comfort. She nursed it day and night until life seemed to glimmer again, though the first sign of life was a cruel, racking cough that shook the child with pain and threatened to take what feeble breath he had. For weeks and weeks this continued, so that life was uncertain for a long time.

Then at last the child seemed to improve, and gradually he was restored to health again. Even so, he was never a strong boy, and the illness appeared to have injured his throat, for as he grew older, he was unable to speak. He understood what was said to him, and he tried hard to answer, but nothing came except a tiny little squeaking sound.

Farmer Carver spoke little to him, but Mrs Carver loved him, and gradually she learnt to understand some of his squeakings, and she began to think about a name for him. A slave always took the surname of his master, but what other name should she give him? She pondered upon "George" for that had been his father's name. Then she thought of George Washington, who had been such a great and good American.

"That'll do," she said. "George Washington

Carver. It's a fine, strong name for a boy."

So the little black orphan was called George Washington Carver. He was a lonely child, for the village was some distance away and there were no children living near the farm. Besides, other children could talk and George could not. He was different from other children. So he wandered alone in the woods and played with the rabbits and squirrels, and watched the tiny insects so busy in the grass. He gathered moss and wild flowers, and dug up plants and seedlings with his brown

fingers, replanting them in the Carver garden where they always grew into something finer and more beautiful. He loved flowers, and flowers always grew for him.

But life was not all gardening. Mrs Carver taught him to wash and cook and do odd jobs about the house. She explained to him that though he had been born a slave, slaves had now been set free throughout the land, and though she was glad to have him, he could leave the farm whenever he wished to do so.

George was happy enough, until at the age of ten he decided that he wanted to go to school. He had tried to teach himself to read from an old reading book, and he could speak a little now, though his voice was still strained and strange. The school for coloured children was quite a long way away, and it charged fees for lessons, so not only would George have to find somewhere else to live, but he would also have to find work to do in the evenings. But he wanted to learn to read and write, so he would have to overcome the difficulties.

Mr Carver agreed to take him to the town on the day before school opened, but when the time came, he was unable to go, so George set out alone. Mrs Carver was sad to see him go—and wondered if he would ever come back again. She watched him walking down the road. He looked more like a seven-year-old than a boy of ten. He was thin and undersized. He carried his few belongings in an old shawl, bundled on a stick, and his smart new shoes were tied together and slung over his shoulder. He was leaving the only home he had ever known, and his heart was sad within him.

That night, in the small town where the school was situated, George looked for somewhere to sleep. He was weary and footsore, homesick and lonely. A large dog sniffed at his bare ankles and followed him round in a friendly way. Soon George found a barn at the back of a house. He crept inside and lay down on the straw. The dog lay down beside him, and George, clutching its paw, found comfort in his loneliness, and fell asleep.

All through the cold, hard winter, he slept in the barn at nights. He did odd jobs for people in the town—running errands, making fires, doing washing, so that he made enough money to pay his school fees and to buy food now and then. Every day he went to school, but he made no friends, for the children laughed at his squeaky voice, and even the teachers found it difficult to understand what he said. Life was very hard, but though George was often hungry and nearly always frozen with the cold, he was beginning to learn the things he wanted to learn. He could read a little and write a little, and he loved to draw on odd scraps of paper. He drew birds and rabbits and flowers and all the things that had made him happy in Diamond Grove.

Then spring came, and with the spring came discovery.

"What are you doing here?" said a voice one evening, for Mr Martin, who owned the barn, had walked into it and seen a thin, brown foot sticking out from the straw. George awoke in terror and began to cry, but Mr Martin was a kind man. He had always been sorry for slaves, and he knew that now they were free, many of them had nowhere to go. So he led George into the kitchen, where he and his wife gave him the first good meal he had eaten for months. And there, with the Martins, George stayed. They gave him a room in a shed. They gave him warmth and food, and in return George did many things for them. He amazed them with his skill at washing and cooking and making fires. He nursed Mrs Martin when

she was ill, and he planted a garden for them—a beautiful garden, where strange, delicate plants seemed to grow at the touch of his fingers.

"He's a bright boy," Mr Martin said, and he helped George with his lessons and often talked to him. He told him of better schools where he might learn even more, for George was doing well at school. So far he knew no geography or history, but his reading was good, and his art wonderful, and in nature study he knew more than the teachers themselves.

For a while all went well. Then the flour mill where Mr Martin worked was closed, and he had to look for

work elsewhere. A job was offered to him in faraway California, and because he was poor he felt bound to take it. This meant leaving George, for there was no money to spare for taking him too. They made arrangements for him to live with neighbours, and they talked to him again about a better school.

George was very sad when the Martins left. He waved goodbye and watched the covered wagon roll away. The Martins had been his friends for nearly three years, and now they had gone.

So a few months later, at the age of thirteen, George took a lift on a mule cart and travelled to Fort Scott. There was a larger school there and he would be able to learn more, for he wanted to learn everything that books could teach him.

The next years were years of great variety. From Fort Scott he moved again to a high school. He did numerous odd jobs in order to keep himself. He worked in hotels and gardens, and during the long summer holidays he wandered from place to place, helping on a ranch, picking fruit in New Mexico, cooking for a gang of men building a railroad. Everyone liked him, for he was willing and hard-working and cheerful. So George saw strange lands, strange scenes, and strange plants that filled his heart with happiness.

Then at last his school days ended.

"I'm free," he thought. "I have saved some money.

I can do whatever I like.—I know! I'll go by train to Diamond Grove and visit the Carvers."

Mr and Mrs Carver were delighted to see him. They were thrilled with his stories and amazed at all he had learned. They were proud indeed of the slave baby who had come to them so near death such a long time before. George slept that night in the log cabin where he had been born. He gazed through the open door at the dark sky merging with the shadows of the Ozark Hills. He had travelled a long way. He had learned many things. What now?

There was only one answer. He must read more books. He must learn more and more.

"I must go to college," said George. "Then, somewhere in the world, there will be great work for me to do."

*   *   *   *   *   *

There *was* great work for him to do. George Washington Carver is remembered today as one of the really great men of America, though his story is too long to be told in full here.

When he went to college, he was refused admission because he was black, but after many years of work he was admitted somewhere else. He wondered what subject in particular he should study. He might take music, for he could play well, and the squeaky voice which had taken so long to be cured, had developed into a fine, singing voice. He might study art, for his paintings were outstanding in their beauty. He might study botany and agriculture, for *his* eyes saw tiny details in nature which other people missed, and the touch of his long, brown fingers brought life to soil and seeds.

So it was as a scientist that he became best known—a scientist who worked with land and trees and flowers, and who persuaded farmers to vary their crops.

"Every year you plant cotton," he said. "Cotton takes all the richness from the earth and gives nothing back. The land needs rest and refreshment. You must now plant something different that will enrich the soil—something like peanuts."

Peanuts! Farmers all over the South planted them. Then they cried,

"What shall we do with them all? They are grown for nothing except pigs' food—or just to be thrown away."

"No," replied Dr Carver. "Nothing in the world need be wasted," and he told them how to use the small, despised peanuts for making coffee, milk, cheese, paper, flour, plastics and boards. He told them how to use peanuts for making over three hundred different products.

He taught farmers how to check disease in fruit, and

A portrait of George Washington Carver

how to prepare wild weeds for nourishing food. He taught them how to save their crops when they were failing. He told them how to make something out of anything, and how to draw the very best out of the land and the gifts that nature had given them. To the poor people of his own race he brought new hope, and to the lands of the Southern States he brought prosperity and new life.

Once a valuable horse had been exchanged for a poor sickly, slave child.

"What a bargain!" Farmer Carver had said bitterly.

It had indeed been a bargain.

A Visit to the Moon

All through the ages people have been curious about the moon. All through the ages they have asked questions about it.

Are there living creatures on the moon? What are they like? How do they live? Can they see our earth spinning in the heavens? Do they ask each other questions about us?

And because until now, no one was able to give satisfactory answers, there have always been stories of imaginary journeys to the moon.

This is a make-believe story, written—just for fun perhaps—by a Frenchman, Cyrano de Bergerac, in 1648. His words have been changed, and a great many left out, for if you were to read the book itself, you would find it very difficult, even in English.

"For many days," he says, "I rose early and collected dew from the grass and the flowers, storing it in the shade in little bottles. When I had a large number of bottles, I tied them about myself and stood out in a field. The heat from the sun drew up the dew, and I found myself rising, rising into the air. So it was that I was able to journey to the moon, where I landed somewhat suddenly in a vast flower-strewn forest.

"I untied the bottles and walked forward. I was in the land of the moon. What should I find?

"Certainly I found beauty everywhere, for birds sang in the trees, and every leaf seemed to echo their songs. All weariness left me. My cheeks grew warm and rosy. My thinning hair became thick, and new blood seemed to rush through my veins making me feel at least fourteen years younger.

"I saw no sign of any inhabitants until I had walked for about ten minutes, when I suddenly came face to face with two enormous animals. One stood staring down at me, but the other disappeared, returning almost at once with seven or eight hundred of the same kind, all of which surrounded me, staring and gaping as if I were indeed the strangest creature they had ever seen.

"I could not, of course, understand their language, but I guessed from their sounds and movements that they were saying,

"'What is it? It cannot be one of us, for it walks on two legs.'

"And I, of course, said to myself,

"'They are certainly not men, for they walk on four legs.'

"Then as I looked more closely, I saw that they *were* men—gigantic men—and, reminding myself that our own babies walk on four legs until we teach them otherwise, I wondered if perhaps that was the natural way to walk, and it was we of the earth who were strange.

"The giant who had found me carried me off to the town, where he took me to his home, put me in a cage, and charged his friends money if they wished to see me. He tied a rope round my neck, and pulled it now and then to make me dance and jump and amuse the company.

" 'What a queer little creature,' everyone seemed to say. 'He's clever too. I wonder what he is and where he came from.'

"Actually I was more clever than they knew, for I soon began to learn their language, of which I found there were two kinds—one for the nobles and one for the common people. The language of the nobles was easy to learn, for it was simply different notes of music, and when their voices were tired, they could carry on the conversation with lutes or other musical instruments. When twenty or thirty men met together to discuss learned things, the result was indeed beautiful—notes, phrases of music and snatches of tunes mingling together in a most harmonious concert.

"The language of the ordinary people was quite different, and was not speech but movement. A movement of a finger, of a hand, of an ear, or a lip, of an arm, of a cheek meant a whole sentence. Other movements meant single words—a stamp of the foot, a wrinkle of the forehead, a shiver of a muscle, and in this way they 'spoke' so quickly that to see a man talking was more like watching him tremble.

"Fortunately for me there was a man in the town who had been born on the sun, and who had travelled upon the earth. Thus, in addition to other languages, he could speak Greek, and as I too, had studied Greek, we were able to speak to each other.

"'I'm very hungry,' I said to him. 'Do you think I could have a meal?'

"'Certainly,' he replied. 'I'll arrange it.'

"He spoke to the man of the house, and I was taken out of the cage and led into a magnificent hall where a servant asked me what I would like.

"'Soup first, if you please,' I replied. At once a wonderful smell of soup stole through the air, and I waited eagerly. After a while, as the soup had not yet appeared, I stood up to go and find it, but the man of the sun said,

"'Where are you going? Why don't you finish your soup?'

"'Finish it?' I cried. 'I have yet to receive the soup and begin upon it.'

"'Oh,' replied the man of the sun, 'of course you don't understand the customs here. You see, people on the moon live only on the smell of food. When meat is cooked, its vapour is stored in a jar. So there are jars of fruit, vegetables—all sorts of things—and the smells are let out a little at a time as they are required.'

"'It seems to me a most unsatisfactory way of eating,' I answered; but after about a quarter of an hour, when I had smelled several courses, I found that I was no longer hungry. Then I remembered that cooks on the earth, though they eat little themselves, are often fatter than other people. Perhaps this is because

they draw more nourishment from the smells of cooking than ordinary people do from eating.

"Although for most of the time I was kept in the cage at the house of the man who had found me, there were occasions when I was taken to other places. Once I was taken to the King's palace, where his most learned doctors examined me, and where the Queen's ladies spent hours on all fours watching me and taking great delight in every movement I made.

"I found that there were two kinds of houses on the moon. One kind was built of very light wood, and stood on four wheels. Sails were fixed to the roof, and when the people wanted a holiday, they spread the sails and sailed away.

"The other type of house could not travel, but could move up and down on a great screw which passed from roof to floor. The house had a large pit beneath it, so that in winter it could be screwed below the ground for warmth, but in summer it could be raised again into the fresh, warm air.

"One day the man of the sun came to my cage and pushed something through the bars, saying,

"'Here are two books for you to read.'

"'Books!' I answered. 'They are very strange books,' for they were more like small boxes. One appeared to be cut from a diamond, and the other from a single pearl.

"When I raised the lids, I saw no pages or printed words, but instead, a number of tiny springs.

" 'These are more like clocks than books,' I thought, and I wondered how to read them. Just then I touched one of the springs, and at once I heard a man's voice speaking in the music-language of the moon.

" 'This is most unusual,' I said to myself. 'A man needs ears, not eyes, for reading in this land, and since there is nothing to learn, then even the smallest children are able to read and write without effort. How clever they must be by the time they grow to manhood.' "

Cyrano de Bergerac's story is very long, but it tells how at last he dropped through space and back on to the earth, where he suddenly found himself lying on a hill in Italy.

"I inquired when a ship would leave for France," he writes, "and when I embarked, my mind was full of my voyage to the moon."

The Girl Who Loved Music

Eileen sat at the piano and played. The music floated out across the field, where the girls of the Loreto Convent were at games.

No one ever had to tell Eileen to practise. She would go over difficult pieces again and again, correcting her own mistakes, playing because she loved to play, playing because she was possessed with an urge to fill the world with music.

It was the 1920's and Eileen was thirteen—a dreamy girl, with red hair and freckles. Her life had not always been as pleasant as this. Born in the Tasmanian Forest, she had wandered with her family to the mainland of Australia, living in tents and shacks, in poverty and hardship. Then, at a convent in a little mining town, the nuns had discovered her gift for music, and it was they who had arranged for her to have a free place as a boarder in Perth, the capital city of Western Australia.

It seemed a long time now since she had come to Loreto. Time passed quickly. A few more years, and school and music lessons would end. She must work now while she had the chance. She must practise and practise.

The door opened, and a voice broke in on her thoughts.

"Eileen," said Sister John, the music teacher, "Wilhelm Backhaus is here. He has agreed to listen to you. Come now."

Eileen stumbled to her feet. Wilhelm Backhaus, the musician! He was famous throughout the world! Her heart beat loudly as Sister John led her to the room where the great man waited, but as soon as she sat at the piano, all her fears left her. She played and played. Then, when she had finished, she put her hands in her lap and swung round on the stool.

Wilhelm Backhaus was silent. He waited till the last soft echoes had blown away on the breeze. Then he leapt to his feet and cried,

"You have a wonderful gift! You must go to Germany at once!"

Eileen's eyes shone with excitement.

"But Eileen's parents are very poor," murmured Sister John.

Backhaus waved his arm as if brushing aside all question of poverty.

"Still she must go to Germany. I will give her introductions in Leipzig," he said.

Then he put his hands on Eileen's shoulders and added.

"You are willing to work hard?"

"Oh, yes," she answered, and her voice was only a whisper. "I don't mind how hard I work or how many hours I practise."

"You see," he said kindly, "you are blessed with a wonderful gift—but what you do with it depends on you alone. You will need to work very hard, and you will need great courage."

Eileen nodded. She understood.

* * * * * *

Within a few weeks a fund was started in Perth, to send Eileen Joyce to Leipzig. The Loreto Convent buzzed with excitement. The girls were delighted to know that their school friend was to have such an opportunity, and thrilled to think that one day she would probably become famous. Eileen laughed and joked with them and was filled in turn with happiness and sadness—happiness at the thought of fulfilling her life-long ambition, and sadness at the knowledge that she must leave her friends and her own country.

Money came steadily into the fund. People of Perth gave donations and collected in various ways, and Eileen herself was given time in the evenings to play at concerts and theatres.

At last nine hundred pounds had been collected, and the date was fixed for Eileen to sail. Mother came to Perth to spend the last few days with her and to see her off. The Loreto girls crowded on the quay and gave her flowers and presents. Then they waved and shouted last-minute messages as the gangway swung up, the ropes were coiled, and the ship began to move.

Eileen stood tearfully on the deck and wished with all her heart that she didn't have to go away. She was still scarcely fourteen years old, so it was no wonder that she felt small and desolate and utterly alone. Mother and the schoolgirls became smaller and smaller until they merged with the harbour and could be seen no more. Australia became fainter and fainter in the distance, until it faded from sight in a hazy blue mist of sea and sky.

And then at last came life in Germany. Eileen had expected that at first she would find it difficult and lonely. But never had she expected it to be as difficult and lonely as this.

She couldn't speak German. She found her lodgings cold and cheerless, and at the College of Music she was thrust into an advanced class with a number of other students. Only a few of them spoke English, and they were all much older than she was. They seemed so grown-up, so clever, that Eileen wondered fearfully if she would ever catch up with them. Her teacher too, a brilliant and rather fierce man, made her nervous, so that her fingers trembled when she played for him and she was unable to show herself at her best.

"I must work," she thought. "I must work." So she practised and practised until her fingers were stiff and her whole body ached. She practised day after day, week after week, month after month.

Gradually she became used to life in Leipzig. Her homesickness became a little more bearable, and she made one or two acquaintances among the students. Sometimes she went to concerts where she listened enraptured to world-famous musicians, and longed to reach their standard of perfection.

By the end of a year she had grown out of her clothes; and her shoes pinched her toes every time she pressed the pedals. She became thinner than ever, for she was nearly always hungry, and she didn't dare to spend much on food. Nine hundred pounds had seemed so much a year ago—but the journey to Leipzig, her lodgings, the expensive lessons at the college had rapidly diminished it.

Then she became ill and had to go into hospital for an operation on her foot. She had to lie in bed and waste weeks of her precious time. When at last she was well enough to practise again, something even worse happened.

A letter came from the people who managed her money, saying that there was only enough left for one more term at the college.

One more term! Eileen was filled with horror. She

had still so much to learn, and only one more term in which to do it. She had gone so far with her studies, and now she could never finish them.

Desperately she worked. There was so much to learn, and time was so short. She must practise. She must practise. She must practise.

Then just at this time, when things were at their very worst, help came. She was standing at the entrance of the concert hall one day, when she dimly heard someone say,

"Oh, Mrs Andreae, may I introduce you to a lonely little Australian?" Half in a dream Eileen was pushed forward to shake hands, and Mrs Andreae and her husband smiled kindly and explained that they were from New Zealand.

"Oh," murmured Eileen, feeling glad to meet someone from her own far-away part of the world.

Mr and Mrs Andreae looked at her in amazement and thought they had never seen such a shabby, ill, uncared-for child. Her ragged, red hair hung untidily round her pale, pinched face, and her dreamy, blue eyes were strained and sad. Her frock was tattered and much too short and thin for the cold German winter, and her shoes were shabby and down at heel. She was a picture of utter weariness and despair.

"Poor little thing," thought Mrs Andreae, but aloud she said, "I wonder if you could find time to have tea with me tomorrow."

Eileen smiled and nodded her head.

"Here's my address," continued Mrs Andreae, handing her a card. "It'll be nice to speak English to someone for a change."

So the next day Eileen went out to tea. She sat on the extreme edge of an armchair and talked shyly about Perth and the Loreto Convent. She answered Mrs Andreae's questions about her studies in Leipzig, and then, quite suddenly, she found herself pouring out all her troubles. Kind Mrs Andreae was full of sympathy and helpfulness.

"You know what *you* want," she said gently—"someone to look after you—and I'm going to be the person to do it."

Eileen looked up in grateful surprise.

"Now listen," continued Mrs Andreae. "Tomorrow I'll take you out and buy you some warmer clothes—and we must do something about your hair. It's a beautiful colour you know, and if you're going to be a famous pianist, we must encourage it to stay within grips or ribbons."

Eileen smiled ruefully.

"Who is your teacher?" asked Mrs Andreae next.

Eileen told her saying,

"I don't seem to get on very well with him. He gets angry with me, and I make mistakes."

"He's a good teacher," replied Mrs Andreae. "But you're probably not really ready for him yet. Have you ever thought of going to Teichmuller?"

"Oh, yes, I went to one of his lectures once. I've always wished that I could have lessons with him."

"Well, we'll see what can be done about it. Just don't worry any more, Eileen. Everything's going to be fine."

Mrs Andreae was as good as her word. She and her husband had taken the "lonely little Australian" straight to their hearts, and nothing was too much trouble for them. They found her a home with a kind German woman, who gave her the good food that she needed and all the mothering that she had missed. They bought her the promised clothes, and best of all they gave her an introduction to the great Herr Teichmuller.

Nervously Eileen let herself be ushered into his presence, but she felt at once his sympathy and understanding, and found it easy therefore to give of her best. She played and played; and Teichmuller, who had heard and taught some of the best pianists of the day, was filled with admiration and the joy of a new discovery. He understood that the child was poor and at the end of her money. Well—what was money? She had a gift, and he would foster it and help her to develop it. He did not want payment.

So a little later Eileen ran out into the windy street, to tell Mr and Mrs Andreae that Herr Teichmuller was going to teach her—and that Herr Teichmuller was quite certain of her power to succeed.

* * * * * *

So Eileen Joyce became one of the most famous pianists in the world, and there were people everywhere who loved to listen to her. They gazed for a moment at her beautiful frocks and her red-gold hair. Then they became lost in the wonder of her playing. And Eileen, as she played, forgot that she was now rich and famous—forgot that she was once poor and ragged. She knew only, as she had always known, that she wanted to make music, and she believed she was put into the world to do just that.

The Story of Parachutes

The story of parachutes began with a dandelion seed floating away on the wind, carried securely by a small umbrella of fine, silken hairs, and dropping gently at last on the earth.

No one knows for how many centuries seeds have used parachutes, but we know that man's attempts to make them have followed more or less his efforts at making balloons and flying-machines. It was fine to fly through the air with engines and wings or gas-filled balloons, but if anything went wrong, there was no escape from death, for any man who fell from a great height fell heavily. He needed, therefore, some device that would resist the wind, bear his weight and allow him to fall slowly and gently.

The first parachute of which any record exists was planned by Leonardo da Vinci in 1514. He made drawings of a huge, flat sail, and wrote careful notes on the way it was supposed to work.

Nearly three hundred years later a Frenchman, Joseph Montgolfier (inventor of balloons), made a small, circular, rigid parachute with a basket hanging beneath it. He put a sheep in the basket and dropped it from the top of a high tower. Slowly and safely the sheep descended to earth.

Other Frenchmen made experiments with rigid

parachutes, and in 1797 a man named Garnerin dropped from a balloon in Paris. Garnerin's parachute was more like those used today, being made of numerous cloth panels forming a cup-shape in reverse, and depending on the wind to open it out. After his success in Paris he decided to give a demonstration in England. The parachute was folded in a long tube shape, with a basket hanging below, and was fixed beneath a balloon.

A huge crowd of people gathered in London to watch. Garnerin rose in the air above them to a height of over two thousand metres. Then he cut the cord that connected him to the balloon. The parachute fluttered open and, though the basket swung wildly during the descent, the Frenchman landed safely.

After that, various people improved the parachute from time to time, until in America, a man named Baldwin designed a folding one made of silk. He made several successful jumps with it, for it opened out as

soon as the air current caught it. The greatest drawback, however, was still the swaying which had been the fault of all the others. One day, after landing, he was talking about this with some of the people in the crowd, when a small boy called out,

"Say! Why don't you make a hole at the top?"

Everyone laughed, but Baldwin said thoughtfully, "That's not a bad idea." In fact it was a very good idea, as Baldwin discovered when he tried it; and parachutes ever since have been made with one or more holes to allow the air pressure to escape, and to keep the parachute in its correct position.

The next great advance in the story of parachutes was also due to an American, Leslie Irvin—later known as Ski-Hi Irvin. His interest in flying began the first time he saw a balloon, and when he was about ten or eleven years old, he made numerous experiments with toy parachutes and small balloons filled with hot air. One day he had a wonderful idea.

"Let's send up a parachute fixed to a hot-air balloon," he explained to his friends. "Then as the hot air cools, the balloon will lose its power, and we shall see if the parachute really works in mid-air."

His friends agreed.

"That will be much more exciting than just throwing parachutes into the air or dropping them from our bedroom windows," they said.

In a short time the parachute was ready, with a load fixed beneath it, and the balloon above. Irvin released the balloon, and it lifted parachute and load into the air. For a few moments everything went well and the parachute sailed eastwards over the fields. Then suddenly the wind changed, and the parachute was borne away to the west, over the Pacific Ocean.

Irvin, however, continued with his experiments, and at the age of fourteen he obtained work on the building of an aeroplane. In the years that followed, he roamed America—car-racing, airship flying, balloon-stunting, high diving, dropping by parachute from aeroplanes—taking in fact, any job that offered danger and excitement.

Now during this time much progress had been made in the construction of aeroplanes, and during the war ending in 1918 many airmen lost their lives when parachutes might have saved them.

When the war was over, America collected every type of parachute, and asked people of all nations to send in designs, so that experts might select the most satisfactory one. Parachutes came from all over the world, and the one that was considered the best in every way came from Ski-Hi Irvin, whose earliest parachute had been carried out to sea.

So far all folding parachutes had been unfolded automatically. A cord was always attached from the parachute to the balloon or aeroplane from which the jump was taken. It was fixed in such a way that the weight of the falling man cut the cord and released the parachute. If, however, the aeroplane had crashed into another, or lost control in any way, the cord often became entangled and prevented the pilot escaping from the aircraft. The safest way would surely be for the airman to release his own parachute when he had fallen into a clear, open patch of sky.

Many experts agreed upon this, and knew it would be possible for a parachute to be packed on a man's back, and to have a short cord which he himself could pull. But there was one great obstacle. People believed that when a man began to fall from the sky, he at once fainted, and therefore could not release his own parachute. Irvin was quite sure that a man did *not* faint. There was only one way to prove it. Someone must take the risk. Someone must jump from an aeroplane and release his own parachute. If the parachute opened, then the man obviously had full command of his powers. If it did not open, then the belief of centuries would be true—and a life would be lost. Who would take the risk? "I will," said Irvin.

So Irvin was taken by plane six hundred metres above the experimental station. He had his parachute strapped on his back, its cord ready for him to pull—*if* he remained conscious. The experts waiting on the field below were filled with fear, but Irvin was calm and confident. He waved once and then jumped. Down through the air he tumbled—hurtling through space.

The crowd stared up at him, so small and far away. Had he fainted? Already he had covered a third of the distance between the plane and the earth. Was he falling to his death?

Ah! Suddenly the parachute opened. Ski-Hi Irvin was still conscious. He had pulled the cord, and the white silk billowed out and brought him slowly and gently through the blue sky, slowly and gently down to earth.

Many parachutes today are still of the Irvin type,

(*Above*) This parachute is being used as a kite. It is attached to a moving car, which pulls it up into the air. (*Opposite*) A parachutist descending by parafoil (see p. 134).

opened by the airman himself, and each one now has a small pilot chute fixed to the top, to pull the parachute away from the man, so that there is no chance of his falling into it. New kinds are attached to weights or dummies, and thrown from aeroplanes for testing, and experiments are being made with parachutes to lower the whole body of a falling plane safely to earth.

Recently, a new form of parachute, called a "parafoil" has been developed. There is a picture of one on page 133 and, as you can see, it looks rather like a large air mattress. It does the same work as a parachute, but instead of dropping straight down to earth it glides slowly and steadily through the air and comes gently down to land. Unlike the ordinary parachute, the parafoil can be steered by pulling on certain of its ropes and it can also be made to bank and turn.

In modern warfare, parachutes are used for landing supplies and equipment, and can carry a weight of as much as 3600 kilograms. In times of peace they are used to bring relief to victims of flood, famine, earthquakes and disease, by dropping food, clothing, medicine, and even doctors and nurses when other means of communication have failed. Parachutes also drop men at forest fires to fight the flames; and they bring supplies to people who are cut off from the outside world by snow and ice.

Hundreds and hundreds of people have saved their

lives with parachutes since Irvin made his historic leap—and there is a special club for people who have done so. It is called the Caterpillar Club, and each member receives a gold caterpillar brooch with his or her name engraved on the back.

"Caterpillar" may seem a strange name for a club whose members have faced death and danger; but caterpillars—ordinary everyday caterpillars—sail out on the summer air on silken threads of gossamer, for caterpillars had parachutes long before man.

And dandelions, of course, probably had parachutes even long before caterpillars.

The Making of a Parachute
Parachutes are always packed very carefully, and inspected once a month. They used to be made of silk, but are now made of nylon. They are not all exactly the same, but an average parachute is made of more than eighty metres of nylon cut into nearly three hundred pieces and stitched together.

The completed circle is seven metres across.

There are twenty-four cords. Each one is more than four metres long, and they are arranged to balance the man comfortably and relieve him of strain.

Parafoils are made of a number of tubes, open at one end and fixed side by side to make a large rectangular shape.

The Flying East Africans

"If you run, you will be shot," said the letter. There were mystery phone calls too. Some of them spoke of rifles, aimed at the track at Meadowbank Stadium in Edinburgh.

But the threats didn't trouble the quiet, gentle Kenyan runner. He wouldn't listen to them.

Already Kipchoge Keino, known to thousands as "Kip", was a legend in athletics. Now he had come to Edinburgh for the 1970 Commonwealth Games. He wasn't afraid to run. Besides, he had to prove that the critics were wrong. They had said that no African would win a medal at the Commonwealth Games. They said that the success of the East African runners at the Mexico Olympics in 1968 had been an accident.

The 1968 Olympic Games were held in Mexico City, at a site over 2300 metres high. Kenyans were used to running in the hills, at a great height; that was why they had won eight medals in Mexico, scoffed the critics. Many people said that the Kenyans would not succeed in Edinburgh, at sea level, where the climate was so different.

Kip Keino and his team-mates set out to prove these people wrong. When the Kenyans arrived in Edinburgh they kept on training. They got up at six to run to the top of Arthur's Seat, the highest hill in the city. Some of the

Kip Keino winning the 1500 metres race at the Commonwealth Games in 1970.

runners found it hard to run in the high winds. But they had trained for years. They knew they would do well.

Kip himself was in fine shape. He was a member of the Kenyan Police Force and his fans called him "the Flying Policeman". He hadn't started to run seriously until he left school. But soon he was well-known as a middle-distance runner. First he was Kenyan champion. Then he competed in the 1964 Olympics. By 1970 he was recognised as the greatest middle-distance runner in the world.

Now he was taking part in the 1500 metres in

Edinburgh. Tense and ready, he waited with the others for the start. Then he was off, running with that long, loping stride, which made it look so easy.

Was he thinking of the death threats? Was he listening for a rifle shot? Was he thinking of the challenge of those who said he wouldn't win?

Kip ran effortlessly, almost as if he were running over the hills in his own country. He had a clear lead and he coasted home, winning the race from New Zealander Dick Quax in 3 minutes 36.6 seconds. The whole stadium rose and cheered as Kip ran a lap of honour. He had set a new United Kingdom record.

Next day the newspapers praised the brave Kenyan. They called him "the incomparable Kip Keino". They talked about his style—"the gliding lope".

But Kip's was not the only Kenyan success of the Games. His team-mate Robert Ouko won the 800 metres and another Kenyan, Charles Asati, won the 400 metres. The Kenyan relay team won the 4 × 400 metres relay.

People began to talk about the East Africans. Clearly their success in Mexico had not just been an accident. They were stronger, faster runners than any other nation. And they made it look so easy!

People compared the Kenyans with another great nation of runners—the Finns. They talked about Hannes Kolehmainen (Hannes the Mighty) and the great Paavo Nurmi, the hero of the 1924 Olympics. He was nicknamed "the Flying Finn".

But why had the Kenyans suddenly come to the fore in the late 1960's? What was the secret of the long, loping stride?

Of course, it hadn't just happened suddenly. Running had always been a great sport in Kenya. Boys like Ouko ran over the hills to school. They had to run long distances, often barefoot, because many of them couldn't afford shoes. Every village had its sports, and athletes from one village or tribe competed against another. But experts noticed that some tribes produced better and faster runners than others. Two major groups of tribes—the Kalenjin and the Kisii—produced many international runners. Why? Experts think it was partly because the people of these tribes lived with their cattle at a great height—usually over 1600 metres. They were used to travelling long distances on foot, through the hills. They ate a diet which included a great deal of meat. This is the right kind of diet for athletes in training.

Some experts also noticed that the Kalenjin had a specially long femur—or thighbone. This meant that a Kalenjin runner had a very long stride. Whatever the secret, there was no doubt about the strength and speed of the Kenyan runners.

In the early 1950's, the Kenya Amateur Athletic Association was formed. From then on, Kenyans competed in world athletics. In 1956, for the first time, Kenya took part in the Olympics. The athletes didn't win any medals, but they gained experience.

In the 1962 Commonwealth Games in Perth, Australia, and in the 1964 Olympics in Tokyo, Kenyans were among the medal winners. They came home in triumph—to a heroes' welcome.

But Kenyan athletes had not yet won any gold medals in the Olympics. Could they do it in 1968 in Mexico? They did—and on the very first day, when Naftali Temu won the 10 000 metres. Kip Keino, already Kenya's best-known runner, won the 1500 metres, and Amos Biwott, who was still just a schoolboy, won the 3000 metres steeplechase.

The Munich Olympics of 1972 brought further successes. Kip Keino won the steeplechase. He hadn't competed seriously in an international steeplechase before.

Kenyan runners took the 4 × 400 relay and a new East African star appeared—John Akii-Bua of Uganda, who not only took the gold medal in the 400 metres hurdles but also set a new world record.

So now the whole world was watching these runners. But those who were looking forward to the 1976 Olympics in Montreal were disappointed. Many had waited eagerly to watch the new generation of East African athletes—men like John Akii-Bua and great middle-distance runners Mike Boit of Kenya and Filbert Bayi of Tanzania.

At the 1964 Olympic Games in Tokyo. The Kenyan athlete, Henry Rono, in the lead during the 400 metres hurdles race.

But a political dispute arose because of New Zealand's sporting links with South Africa. In protest, black African countries refused to take part in the Games. So the Olympics of 1976 were a sad disappointment.

All of the time, new East African athletes were emerging. Kip Keino had now retired from international competitions. He was in charge of physical education at the Kenya Police College. There he spotted many talented young runners. The Kenyan Army and the Prison Service also produced top class athletes.

East African athletes. (*Opposite*) John Akii-Bua, winner of the 400 metres hurdles, Munich, 1972. (*Below*) Filbert Bayi. (*Right*) Mike Boit.

But East African countries boycotted the 1980 Olympics too. These Olympics were held in Moscow. Only the Ethiopians kept up the tradition of East African runners. Miruts Yifter, who was already thirty-five years old and was running against much younger men, won the 10 000 metres. The newspapers called it "a remarkable race". He won easily—and went on to win another gold medal in the 5000 metres.

The Ethiopians were also becoming famous as long-distance runners. Soon they were to compete in marathons all over the world.

But what about the future? A top Kenyan coach has said, "There are hundreds of runners in Kenya, waiting to be discovered."

Now training begins in secondary schools. National school championships are held every year. A promising young runner gets a great deal of help from older athletes and school coaches. East Africa is proud of its young athletes.

In a little over twenty years East African runners have come a long way—from village sports to international acclaim.

Anne Forsyth